D0908609

THE LEADERSHIP GENIUS
OF JULIUS CAESAR

THE LEADERSHIP GENIUS
OF JULIUS CÆSAR

Modern Lessons from the Man
Who Built an Empire

PHILLIP BARLAG

Berrett–Koehler Publishers, Inc.
a BK Business book

BERRETT-KOEHLER PUBLISHERS, INC.

1333 Broadway, Suite 1000, Oakland, CA 94612-1921
Tel: (510) 817-2277   Fax: (510) 817-2278   www.bkconnection.com

ORDERING INFORMATION

Quantity Sales. Special discounts are available on quantity purchases by corporations, associations, and others. For details, contact the "Special Sales Department" at the Berrett-Koehler address above.

Individual Sales. Berrett-Koehler publications are available through most bookstores. They can also be ordered directly from Berrett-Koehler:
Tel: (800) 929-2929; Fax: (802) 864-7626; www.bkconnection.com

Orders for College Textbook/Course Adoption Use. Please contact Berrett-Koehler: Tel: (800) 929-2929; Fax: (802) 864-7626.

Orders by U.S. Trade Bookstores and Wholesalers. Please contact Ingram Publisher Services, Tel: (800) 509-4887; Fax: (800) 838-1149; E-mail: customer.service@ ingrampublisherservices.com; or visit www.ingrampublisherservices.com/Ordering for details about electronic ordering.

Berrett-Koehler and the BK logo are registered trademarks of Berrett-Koehler Publishers, Inc.

PRINTED IN THE UNITED STATES OF AMERICA

Berrett-Koehler books are printed on long-lasting acid-free paper. When it is available, we choose paper that has been manufactured by environmentally responsible processes. These may include using trees grown in sustainable forests, incorporating recycled paper, minimizing chlorine in bleaching, or recycling the energy produced at the paper mill.

LIBRARY OF CONGRESS CATALOGING-IN-PUBLICATION DATA

Name: Barlag, Phillip, author.
Title: The leadership genius of Julius Caesar : modern lessons from the man who built an empire / Phillip Barlag.
Description: Oakland, CA : Berrett-Koehler Publishers, [2016] | Includes bibliographical references.
Identifiers: LCCN 2016021763 | ISBN 9781626566934 (hardcover)
Subjects: LCSH: Caesar, Julius. | Leadership--Case studies. | Heads of state--Rome--Case studies. | Generals--Rome--Case studies.
Classification: LCC HD57.7 .B36636 2016 | DDC 658.4/092--dc23
LC record available at https://lccn.loc.gov/2016021763

FIRST EDITION

21 20 19 18 17 16   10 9 8 7 6 5 4 3 2 1

Interior design: VJB/Scribe   *Edit:* Elissa Rabellino
Cover design: Wilsted & Taylor   *Index:* Paula C. Durbin-Westby
Production service: Linda Jupiter Productions   *Proofread:* Henrietta Bensussen

For my father, Bruce, who is always
in my corner, above all else

CONTENTS

TIMELINE OF KEY EVENTS IN
CAESAR'S LIFE AND CAREER

100 BC   Born in Rome.

81   Refuses Sulla's order to divorce his wife; goes on the run.

80–78   Early military service; wins civic crown.

75   Travels east to study under masters of rhetoric; captured by pirates.

72   Elected as military tribune.

69   Elected as quaestor.

65   Elected as aedile.

63   Conspiracy of Catiline; elected as pontifex maximus.

62   Serves as praetor; finds an angry mob ready to riot on his behalf.

61–60   Serves as governor of Spain, chooses between triumph or consulship.

59   First consulship; formation of triumvirate with Crassus and Pompey.

58   Beginning of proconsulship; defeats Ariovistus.

55   Bridges the Rhine, first invasion of Britain.

54   Second invasion of Britain, death of daughter and mother.

53   Crassus killed in battle against the Parthians.

52   War with Vercingetorix culminates in the siege of Alesia.

49   Crosses the Rubicon; the Civil War begins.

48   First dictatorship; second consulship; defeats Pompey in Greece; wins surrender of superior naval squadron; Pompey murdered in Egypt.

47   Stops a rebellion in Italy with one word; campaigns in North Africa.

46   Third consulship.

In my professional life, I have the extraordinary honor and privilege to be witness to some of the most fascinating business conversations in the world. For almost a decade, I've had the chance to sit and listen to some of the world's most accomplished, C-level executives from top-tier companies share their perspective on what they've done right as well as that with which they struggle. To me, these executives who run large, complex corporate functions of global companies are luminaries. I often joke that I am the one person who doesn't belong in every room I'm in because I'm not at that level and don't claim to be. I simply help facilitate the discussions.

After nearly a decade of listening to these discussions, something struck me: The challenges that executives address are always the same things, over and over. When I look back, a clear pattern emerges. Whether the markets are thriving or near collapse, at the heart of the executive agenda is leadership effectiveness. More specifically, executives are always seeking ways to build better teams and be better leaders.

A funny thing happened to me a few years ago. Following nothing more than general interest, I began reading a lot about ancient Rome, in general, and Julius Caesar, in particular. I didn't know much about the guy at first. I knew he was ruthless, ambitious, a dictator, and he died a bloody death on the Ides of March. But with each page I read, I discovered that he was so much more interesting than what my cursory knowledge of history suggested. What is more, it struck me that Caesar uncovered truths about leadership that shed genuine light on the very modern, here-and-now business discussions I come across on a daily basis. Imagine my surprise when I realized that the one person who could answer some of the seemingly unanswerable leadership questions of today's top-performing executives had been dead for over two thousand years.

Caesar was truly a genius, and he packed several lifetimes of adventure, intrigue, drama, and daring into his fifty-five years. What was most surprising to me about him was that his leadership style was modern, so much so that the insights into leadership that propelled him to glory are just as spot-on relevant today.

The more I learned about Julius Caesar, the more I came to appreciate the depth of his humanity. At each stage of his career, he used his understanding of human nature masterfully to grow his power base.

Human nature doesn't change all that much. We have basically the same "operating system" as the people in Caesar's day. The only thing that has changed between then and now is the social context. Simply by reading up on the life and career of Caesar, I have gained priceless insights into leadership. With this book, I hope to pass on some of those timeless lessons by applying them to a modern social context. Oh, and there are pirates, and who doesn't love pirates?

INTRODUCTION

This is a book about Julius Caesar and what he means to modern leaders. It is not a biography, and it is not intended to be a history book in the traditional sense. There are plenty of such works out there, and for me to try to re-create them would be a waste of my time—and yours. Besides, I'm not a historian. I just like history.

It struck me that for as many great books on Caesar as there are, they all explore Caesar in his own time. There is very little written to help us answer the questions "So what? What does any of this mean to me all these years later?"

Historians and academics certainly spend considerable energy discussing—and often arguing about—the true nature of Caesar's character. But one thing about the great man never comes up for debate: he was an exceptionally effective leader. There is a wonderful historiography for Caesar, a wealth of great books and articles, each adding its own color to the canvas that makes up the picture of his life. But there's nothing quite like this out there: a look at Caesar as a leader through modern eyes. This book explores not just who Caesar was but how we can take the blueprint of leadership he gave us to be better leaders in our own time. Caesar was a lot of things: politician, statesman, general. Now let us add "teacher" to that list.

As we explore the leadership genius of Caesar, it is worth noting the violence that hung in the air like a putrid fog, permeating every aspect of Roman life. One of the best ways to seal your fate in ancient Rome was to try to cut into the advantages that the oligarchy held tightly. Caesar entered the political landscape with a controversial reform agenda, one that was sure to be brutally suppressed by the senatorial order. It was a violent time, and it would take someone of extraordinary talent to get anything visionary accomplished. That he succeeded in implementing his agenda and consolidating all the power in Rome for himself proves his mettle as a leader. What was it about this guy that made him such a phenomenal leader, and what—if anything—does that mean to us all these centuries later? These simple questions are the heart of this book.

One last note about the organization of the book: I have picked and chosen events from Caesar's life to explore his revolutionary leadership style and point out the modern leadership lessons that his extraordinary life offers us today. A historian reading this book might be frustrated by its asymmetry (and its lack of chronology). Some things that are of great historical importance have been overlooked, while other, more minor events are amplified to highlight the leadership lessons they teach us. The focus of this book also means that some people and events that deserve study or that have a role to play in a more complete historical narrative have been left behind. (Sorry in advance, Clodius!) All of this is in service of my main goal: extracting the great lessons from Caesar's career that we can use to become better leaders today.

1

LEAD WITH POWER, NOT FORCE

There are two ways to lead an organization: by power or by force. The first way creates the shortest distance between leaders and their goals—but it is much harder. For this reason, many leaders default to the use of force.

Power is the ability to intrinsically motivate people to act in the way you want them to. You tap into their hearts and minds, and they follow you because they want to. Having true power means that the team becomes an extension of the will of the leader. This is the ultimate goal for any leader, and this is what Julius Caesar was able to achieve.

Conversely, force is the use of external threats or pressure to compel action. Leadership by force is of questionable effectiveness and certainly cannot be sustained over a period of time. If someone falls in line with a course of action because they fear for their job, then they aren't really being led; they are being pushed. This is actually despotism, and it is just as prevalent in the modern organization as it was in the ancient world. It isn't true leadership, but it's a lot easier.

Through human history, force has been the default leadership style. As we try to break free from the historical pull of force, let us consider one of the greatest examples of a leader who understood the critical distinction between power and force. For his ability to connect with people in a genuine way, for his mastery in unlocking the intrinsic motivation of those in his organization, and for his demonstration of the triumph of power over force, there is no better leadership role model than Julius Caesar. Very few people so innovative, so ahead of their time, could break the mold and so decisively follow such an unknown path.

$\backsim$

It was 47 BC. Julius Caesar stood before his army, the most powerful that Rome had ever assembled. For fifteen years they had marched through Europe, fighting Germans, Gauls, and even other renegade Roman armies. They had crossed the English Channel to become the first Romans to encounter the mystical and terrifying island to the north. They had followed their commander to the ends of the earth, defeated every enemy, and stared down death. Now they were back on the Italian peninsula and in open revolt.

The time had come to call due all of Caesar's promises: back pay, land to farm, an end to endless campaigning, and no more fighting other Romans. These were the incentives he had used to keep his army motivated. But conquest after conquest came and went, and they were always just one more victory away. Enough was enough.

At first the army simply refused to march on. Then inaction turned to discontent, and resentment boiled over into fury. The deadliest army in the world cut itself loose from its moorings, angry and leaderless, and whipped itself into a frenzy. Thousands of soldiers from the most elite fighting unit in world history rose up. Instead of fighting foreign enemies, the army ravaged its own. They began turning against the citizens they were sworn to protect and against their commander.

It didn't happen all at once; the mood of the army had grown sour steadily over some time. During most of this insurgency, Caesar wasn't with his men, however. He was in Egypt floating down the Nile on a pleasure cruise with the charming queen of Egypt, Cleopatra. While taking his ill-timed vacation, Caesar had turned over command of the army camped in Italy to his lieutenant, Marc Antony, who lacked Caesar's charisma and leadership skill. It did not take Marc Antony long to lose control, and with Caesar in Egypt, Antony failed to stem the tide of sinking morale.

Once Caesar learned of the critical situation back home, he wasted no time returning to Italy to confront his troops. Without pausing to gather bodyguards or take any precautions for his personal safety, he marched straight to the front of his troops and quietly and confidently took the podium. If he was anxious as he faced his army, he didn't show it. Standing before thousands of trained killers who in the last days and weeks had savaged the surrounding area, he remained calm and stone-silent. He stood at the head of his army until all of his troops fell into quiet respect for their commanding officer. Before he had even spoken a word, he had leveled the playing field.

Caesar uttered one simple word. Then he fell silent, letting his single utterance permeate the air. At first the soldiers were confused. Was he only going to say just one word to address their grievances? And then the weight of the word sank in.

"Citizens."

Caesar didn't use force, bringing in other troops to suppress the revolt. He didn't threaten violence or use intimidation to take back control. No, Caesar used his power to intrinsically motivate his army. He tapped into the collective psyche of his army and found a way to remind them that they wanted to stay in his good graces. He didn't tell them to stop their revolt; he gave them the necessary information to allow them to choose for themselves, a much more sustainable and authentic decision.

With that one word, the revolt was over. But what was so magical about it? How could any leader have so much authority, so much gravitas, that he could break the murderous resolve of a treasonous army with such little effort?

We will explore the extent of Caesar's leadership power in a moment, but this little footnote from more than two thousand years ago points to something often missed in looking back at history. We neglect—to our detriment—the leadership lessons that history affords us. Caesar was a transformative figure in history. He was, and still is, truly largely than life. But lost in the fantastic stories of the extraordinary man is the very real, very relevant set of lessons that he offers leaders today. With Caesar, we find many layers of relevance and insight. His subtle and brilliant leadership mastery still matters now, to anyone seeking to lead an organization, a team, or a change management agenda.

In many ways, Caesar foreshadowed the archetype of the modern, enlightened, and progressive leader. Yes, he was absolutely a product of his times, and those times reflected different values and ways of doing things. Not everything

Caesar said and did should be taken as a literal example of how to lead in the modern world. But he was so far ahead of his own time, so different, so brilliant, that he closes the leadership gap between then and now more than anyone else who has ever lived.

Year in and year out, millions of people pore over the latest business best-seller lists for the next leadership book to read or wait for the next edition of *Harvard Business Review* for the latest dispatches by some management luminary. Often the concepts these authors present are very insightful, but just as often, they are drawn from an individual's personal experiences and lack analysis and objectivity.

Through temporary trends and fleeting concepts, the search continues for the sound principles and durable techniques of leadership. But trends and concepts come and go. History endures.

The lessons of history should not be the exclusive domain of historians. Modern leaders seeking to up their game should look to whatever sources of insight they can find, even when those sources might be a little unorthodox. The history of civilization, after all, is the history of leadership. It might seem strange to imagine Julius Caesar strutting into a boardroom or developing a human capital strategy, but his actions and abilities can and should inform us in such endeavors today.

The very name of Caesar has come to be cloaked in myth and folklore. Everyone knows his name, but what do we really know about him as a man, as a leader, as someone who actually lived and breathed, and walked the same earth as we all do?

Caesar was a transformative leader. He lived in a violent and tumultuous time, rising through Roman society because he possessed unique and innate abilities as a leader. What separated Caesar from the pack was that he understood the important distinction between power and force. While history is full of examples of those who ruled with an iron fist, Caesar went in a different direction, unlocking the hidden motivation of those he sought to lead so that they chose to follow. In doing so, he set the blueprint for leadership that we seek in great leaders today. By going back in time to study Caesar in his own time, we are going back to the birth of modern leadership. In some ways, you could say that Julius Caesar invented modern leadership.

Caesar's career bubbled over with adventure, intrigue, drama, tension, and seduction. There had never been anyone like him before, nor has there been anyone like him since. But he was a man, a flesh-and-blood human being, and he had quirks and faults to go with all of his genius and gravitas.

He was ambitious, vain, and quite possibly manic. His energy level was extraordinary, and more than two thousand years after his death, we can still feel its reverberations. It has been said that Caesar could simultaneously dictate letters to numerous scribes at once. The image of Caesar, in his command tent at the front of a life-and-death battle, dictating four letters to four scribes at the same time and having each one turn out beautifully, held up as an example of the height of Latin prose, is a telling visual of the kind of person he was. His mind was meticulously organized, and he would most likely be described as having a photographic memory today.

But unlike many people with long memories, Caesar was not prone to holding a grudge. On the contrary, in an age when people got all crazy about their honor and prestige, Caesar could easily forget a slight. In fact, he often used this ability to "let it go" to his advantage, showing himself to be a gracious and clement leader, and winning power and loyalty in the process. While his contemporaries often used office or authority to murder adversaries, Caesar won them over with charm, forgiveness, and magnanimity.

Caesar was one of those people who were good at everything they tried. Through his early career, he worked at and refined his skills, but he was building off of a foundation of talent that was staggering. He was as good in one-on-one situations as he was delivering a speech in front of huge crowds. His command of language was exceptional, and he was equally gifted in speaking as in writing. Pliny the Elder, a Roman naturalist and historian, framed his description of Caesar by saying, "I will not speak here of his energy and steadfastness, or of his sublime ability to comprehend everything under the sun, but of the vitality he possessed and the fiery quickness of his mind."

In his book *Caesar: A Biography*, historian Christian Meier lauds Caesar's quick wit and his ability to pick up new ideas and concepts with remarkable speed. Caesar was adaptable, able to move in and out of various circumstances and social situations with tremendous ease. And despite the steadfastness of Caesar's conviction, Meier says, "there was a playfulness about him, an almost youthful profusion of potentialities." He used humor in a calculated way, defusing tense situations with laughter before things got too far.

Underneath his good-natured veneer, Caesar was deadly serious about getting what he wanted, but he was never insensitive to the goals and needs of the people around him. In fact, he had a unique ability to reconcile his goals with those of his contemporaries and to forge mutually beneficial plans or proposals. Besides, he knew that humorless people wear on those around them and that being too serious would eventually diminish the interest of others to work with him. His colleague and committed opponent Cato never learned that lesson, and most modern books refer to him with words like "stodgy" and "humorless." Caesar saw no advantage in being a wet blanket, so he tended to keep things light as a first line of defense.

For Caesar, anything was possible; it was simply a matter of will and determination. In modern terms, we would say that Caesar had grit, that essential resolve to see something through once his mind was set upon an action or an outcome.

Historians often write about the audacity of his actions. For example, he had affairs with countless married women, including the wives of critical political allies. Certainly this was less shocking in ancient Rome than it would be today, but nevertheless, it's eye-opening that he did so with such amazing frequency.

Caesar was certainly vain. Fastidious in his appearance, he looked for ways to push boundaries in dress and appearance. As a young man, he scandalized older conservatives by—*gasp!*—wearing his belt loosely. As he got older, his hairline retreated up his scalp, and it seemed to bother him immensely. Some have credited him with the invention of the comb-over.

In a modern sense, it's easy to imagine getting a drink with him and discussing anything from politics to fashion, sports to science. He was a polymath, interested in everything, and yet deeply accessible to anyone and everyone around him. His contemporaries found him irresistible. There were times in his career when his opponents didn't want to be around him, lest they find themselves unable to resist his charms and come to some sort of an accommodation. If Caesar were plucked from the ancient world and dropped into our own, he would assuredly survive and thrive. One can only imagine that it wouldn't take long for Caesar to rise through the ranks and become a CEO.

Caesar was born into complicated times, with Rome transitioning from one system of government to another. In fact, in many ways, he was the fulcrum of the lever on which that shift happened. His career and life will never cease to be fascinating, and for our benefit, they will always have lessons to teach. For example, in that one word—*citizens*—the layers of learning are deep and multifaceted. Why was it so darned effective? Let's dive back in.

Back to Caesar's deafening single word. It was disarmingly simple. It took a moment for the gravity of this word to sink in, and its impact cannot be understood without some brief context.

Caesar was a member of the Julii family, one of Rome's most ancient and revered lineages, which traced its ancestry all the way to the goddess Venus herself. To be a Julii was thought to have been literally descended from the gods. As head-scratching as that may seem to us today, Caesar's troops believed it, and whether Caesar believed it or not, he sure went out of his way to remind people of his divine origins.

But despite his godly lineage, Caesar had long projected an image to his troops as a common man. He marched beside them. He ate with them in the mess hall and shared many of their hardships. The contrast between how he acted and how he would have been expected to act was not lost on his troops; they loved him for it. To signify the close bond, Caesar called his men *comrades*—a much more powerful term than *citizens*. Outside of the army camps, class and family lineage mattered, but when they were responsible for each other's lives, Caesar—unique among the leaders of his time—and his soldiers were equals. His choice of the word *comrade* was deliberate. It engendered loyalty.

When confronted with the rebellion of the army, Caesar's use of the word citizens told his men that they were no longer his army. Caesar was saying, "You're not my soldiers anymore. You don't belong in my army. I don't need you. You are average Roman citizens." When the troops came to realize what he had said, they were devastated. Gone was the bond forged over fifteen years of fighting together. Gone was their shared destiny. And—perhaps most important—gone was their equality. With one word, Caesar had asserted his social, political, and moral authority. He had evoked the Roman class system and reminded them of the contrast between himself and them.

For the men of Caesar's army, the weight of this authority coming down on them at once was crushing. It broke their resolve. The army began to cry out, begging for forgiveness. They couldn't bear the thought of losing their special status as comrades with Caesar, descendant of the exalted goddess Venus.

When his men cried out, Caesar ratcheted up the pressure. They could have all their banal demands. He would get a new army—one that he would anoint with his lineage. He would finish the civil wars and bring peace to Rome, and that army was the one that would be steeped in glory, honor, wealth, and prestige.

The revolt crumbled into dust; it was dead, done in by the power of one word. The army begged to be forgiven and returned to their privileged status. They begged to be punished. They begged to get back to work.

At first, Caesar pretended to be indifferent to their cries. Eventually, he "allowed" himself to be persuaded. One more campaign together, he vowed, and then they would have all that had been promised and more: land, money, and glory—and, most important, they could retire as his veterans, his favorites, his comrades. And so promised, so done. Shortly after, they sailed for North Africa and crushed the last significant opposition in the civil war. Caesar was now the undisputed and sole ruler of Rome.

LEAD WITH AN UNDERSTANDING
OF HUMAN NATURE

The nature of power is often misunderstood. The secret to Caesar's genius as a leader lay in his unique insight into what power really is, and what it is not.

With one word, Caesar disarmed an armed insurrection and proved his brilliance as a leader. Not through force of arms but through power, he unlocked the motivation within his army to choose on their own to continue to follow him. Any other leader of the time would have raised fresh troops and come storming in, guns (or spears, rather) blazing. Caesar's only armor was his understanding of human nature. It was all he needed.

In antiquity, the use of force was the simplest way to get people to act. Staring down the razor-sharp tip of a sword has a way of narrowing your field of vision, making anything else within your line of sight insignificant by comparison. It is also pretty effective at influencing a decision. A sword says, "Do what I say or bleed." It sends a very compelling message.

While most of us won't literally stare down the wrong end of a sword in our careers, there are certainly modern equivalents of force, such as the fear of not getting a much-deserved promotion or, worse, losing one's job. In this sense, the threat of force is still a looming presence in the modern business world and is still deployed by leaders as they seek to pursue their agendas.

It is power that is at the heart of great leadership, not force. Actions compelled through force may yield the desired result in the short term and may even be required in rare circumstances. But usually, the use of force creates resentment and sows the seeds of discord. Many high-profile leaders have met their demise, both literally and figuratively, because the collective resentment from the use of force built up into full-fledged revolt. Dictators have been toppled, CEOs have been sacked, and incumbents have been ousted because they failed to master this subtle but important distinction.

It's important to note that few leaders in history relied exclusively on power over force. Mahatma Gandhi and Mother Teresa stand out in large measure because they are the exceptions. We shouldn't think of the leadership technique of power as the complete absence of the use of force. Rather, the takeaway should be that the most effective, long-term way to lead people is through the cultivation of power.

With Caesar, we find many layers of relevance and insight into how to lead an organization, a team, or a change management agenda. The truth of who Julius Caesar really was and how he led is even better than the mythology or the poetry of Shakespeare. The events of his life are extraordinary indeed, and he compiled a career more colorful and accomplished than any other leader to date. And he did so by using power over force. Throughout this book, we will cut through the fog and folklore to get to know this man as the extraordinary leader he was, and to let him be our guide in understanding the true nature of power over force.

2

LEAD FROM THE FRONT

Intransigence is something that even the most beloved leader faces at some point in their career.

Every leader confronts a time when their organization does not want to move forward. Morale is sinking, competition is fierce, and times are tough. When that happens, what example will you set? Will your team be able to look to you to see how to act, what to do?

Caesar showed that leading by example is the best form of leadership—that personal commitment and courage matter more than force or fierce words. Perhaps no story from Caesar's colorful life so poignantly demonstrates the power of leading from the front than the Battle of Munda.

Leadership grounded in power is moral leadership. It is based not only on people's actions but also on their values—*why* they do things, not just *what* they do. Leading from the front is a critical component of moral leadership. For Caesar, his actions in Munda gave him the moral leverage he needed to unlock his organization's motivation.

❧

"No" was not something Caesar heard very often, especially from his army. Openly defying his orders, his men folded their arms and refused to advance. It infuriated the great commander.

Caesar tore off his helmet and cast it aside. He wanted to be sure his army had their eyes on him, their leader, and what he was about to do. If he had to die to prove a point, then he would, and he wanted them all to see it happen.

It was 45 BC. His army was exhausted. They had marched relentlessly to catch the enemy, and rather than give them time to rest, Caesar ordered the men to charge once again. At first they obeyed, surging toward an army of nearly twice as many soldiers. As they came within throwing distance, their enemy let loose a volley of javelins—six-foot-long, solid-wood shafts tipped by big iron points honed to a remorseless, razorlike sharpness. As the volleys fell on Caesar's troops, many in the front lines fell. Scared, tired, and surrounded by dead comrades, the advance ground to a halt.

Defying his commands to advance, this army, unusually timid in the face of an enemy position, was not budging. It was surely sweltering in the Spanish sun, with the heavy burden of armor and equipment, but that was better than charging headlong into certain death. For Caesar, the situation was critical. It was time to move; there could be no more delay. What could he do? How could one man compel an entire army to overcome its obstinacy and attack?

Pushing his way forward from the safety of the rear, Caesar sized up his army. A typical Roman response would have been to make an example out of a few malcontents, to order the beating or death of a few to send a message to the many. Caesar's contemporaries would have deemed such a course of action justified, if not expected. But Caesar was different.

That wasn't how he led. What good would come from exacting a leader's vengeful prerogative? The army still wouldn't want to advance, and they would resent him to boot. For Caesar, it was clear. If his army wouldn't attack, then he would. By himself.

After shedding his helmet and making sure that they saw him clearly, Caesar questioned the bravery of his soldiers. He then turned around and charged headlong uphill toward the enemy army. Alone. One Roman general, sword in hand, running unprotected to take on an entire army.

Caesar led by example, even in the face of death. If he wanted his army to act, then he knew that he had to expect the same of himself. He had to lead from the front. With each step, he moved farther away from the safety of his own men and closer to his destiny. His enemies must have been giddy seeing him approach, his own men dumbfounded. In just a few steps he was within range of the enemy's javelins, and they let loose a massive volley, hundreds of deadly weapons, all zeroed in on one target. As the shower of spears reached their apogee and arced toward their descent, the life of the greatest leader of his age—and perhaps of any age—hung in the delicate balance between luck and gravity.

Caesar's one-man attack shook his men out of their torpor. As the javelins plunged toward their target, the army frantically rushed forward to keep up with their commander. Shamed into action through his courage, they charged with frenzy. The men advanced hard on the heels of their general, and they quickly overtook him, engaging the enemy and allowing Caesar the cover of his soldiers. But Caesar didn't fade to the safety of the rear. He continued to fight, hand to hand, wielding his sword in the thick of the bloody fighting.

Caesar ducked, dodged, and used his shield to maximum effect. Somehow, all the spears missed their mark, and he was unscathed. When one was lucky, it was considered to be demonstrable proof of the favor of the gods, and certainly Caesar had been lucky beyond measure. His army witnessed an entire volley of spears, each pointed directly at him, fall harmlessly to the earth. The gods were on his side because he led from the front, and his army was on his side, too.

Caesar's army claimed victory after a gruesome day of fighting. Their pride and honor were restored and morale surged. Most important, their devotion to their leader reached even greater depths. Caesar famously stated that at previous battles, he had fought for victory, but at this one, he fought for his life. Rather than beat or bully his men into action, he put his own life on the line to demonstrate his commitment to the cause that he was asking them to pursue.

LEAD FROM A POSITION OF CREDIBILITY

Tense and complex situations often create a desire in leaders to insulate themselves. To be uncertain or afraid in difficult situations is not the mark of bad leadership; it's the mark of humanity. Leading from the front takes courage, which, as the Battle of Munda showed, Caesar had in spades.

People want to know that their leader has skin in the game. They want to see that the leader is right there with them in the trenches, fighting the same battle. Being insulated from an organization erodes a leader's moral credibility. On the other hand, leading from the front builds moral credibility. It gives you the opportunity to create a common will and to demonstrate good faith to your organization. If a leader is willing to put their life—or in modern terms, their career—on the line during a critical moment, then the team is much more likely to want to join in the fight. Better to fight and lose together than to be divided and suffer the consequences.

The test of leadership is not the absence of fear. Rather, it is in the ability to overcome that fear at the critical moment and lead from the front. In the course of his life, Caesar built a leadership persona that demonstrates the importance of leading from the front. Not only can this create a moral lever with which to unlock the motivation of an organization, but also it can serve as a point of contrast with the competition, as the next story shows.

♂

It was 48 BC. With the fate of the Roman world in the balance, the armies of two great generals were engaged in a life-and-death struggle off the coast of Greece. During a decisive battle at a town called Pharsalus, Caesar was in the fray, issuing commands and orchestrating movements, every bit the dashing general. As the day swung toward Caesar and his army, his rival and antagonist Pompey fled the field. Rather than try to rally his flagging army, Pompey sneaked away, abandoning his men to their fate, and fled east toward Egypt.

Never one to miss such an opportunity, Caesar left his army in the command of lieutenants and took off in hot pursuit of Pompey. While he was in a boat crossing the Hellespont (the modern Dardanelles), a squadron of naval vessels loyal to Pompey appeared on the horizon. Rather than flee the massively superior force, Caesar took his small craft and headed straight for the enemy flagship. He boarded the vessel and confronted the commander of the squadron. Underscoring the results of the battle, and comparing his courage with Pompey's cowardice, he demanded and won their complete surrender.

Pompey's retreat from Pharsalus had undermined the loyalty of his many military units. Why fight Caesar if their commander wouldn't fight for them? On the other hand, Caesar's men had no doubt that if the roles were reversed, their leader would be standing right beside them.

Pompey's refusal to lead from the front ended up contributing to Caesar's growing strength, as Caesar was able to swing one of Pompey's naval units to his side. Certainly there was a degree of risk involved in Caesar's action. He put himself right at the feet of an enemy commander. But this was a calculated risk. Caesar's demand for surrender came on the heels of his adversary's abandonment of his army. He made the call that the timing was right to assert himself, not only in front of his soldiers but in front of his adversaries as well. In this case, the benefits of leading from the front extended beyond the borders of his own organization and into the camp of the enemy.

In the two stories in this chapter—the death charge up the hill and demanding the surrender of a vastly superior force—Caesar gives us a template for effective leadership. Lead from

LEAD FROM THE FRONT

the front like Caesar to build your moral authority and your power base.

If we do not heed the importance of leading from the front, then we run the risk of allowing doubt and apprehension to creep into the organization. Leading from the front may push us outside of our comfort zones, but it will most certainly help us attain greater heights.

As Caesar showed, leading from the front is best deployed in moments of fear and doubt, when the organization is having a hard time executing or when morale hits a low. These moments, when the temptation to issue stern commands creeps in, are when leadership from the front has the most effect.

Power is not given; it is earned. A leader's willingness to lead from the front goes a long way in forging a base of power. What is more, power erodes if not cultivated. By judiciously choosing the right times to step to the front, you can shore up your power base for the future.

3

DEFY CONVENTION

Tradition matters to people; the modern world is no different than the ancient one in this regard. But being a man or woman apart has a distinct advantage in building a leadership base. Defying convention does not mean being disrespectful to tradition; it means not being subservient to it past the point of reason. Too often, leaders fail to make this distinction.

Like so many of us, leaders in Caesar's time were often faced with the choice of doing what they thought was right or going with the flow. By continually defying convention, Caesar proved himself to be a man with conviction, an innovative thinker, and a fighter for the people. In the next story, Caesar shows how doing what you believe to be right can further your reputation as a principled leader, as the kind of leader that others want to follow.

He had not been accused of treason outright, but rumors had begun to swirl that he had been involved in a conspiracy against the state. Such whispers could take on a life of their own and turn deadly in ancient Rome. Treason was taken seriously; to be convicted meant death. For some, simply to be accused was enough to separate a head from its shoulders.

It was 63 BC. Gossip and innuendo worked much the same then as they do now. Petty people engaged in office politics, whispering lies or half-truths that spread like wildfire, getting more shocking with each iteration. The haughty senatorial class reveled in salacious gossip, especially when the target was an outsider like Caesar. There were plenty of people who wanted the rumors to be true, people who would delight in the fall from grace of this ambitious up-and-comer. Then, as now, petty rivals were on the hunt for any ammunition to use against the object of their enmity.

The Senate had been called into emergency session to discuss the Catiline conspiracy that had been brought to light a few weeks earlier. The conspiracy was the result of the slow-building, seething frustration of Catiline, a senator with more ambition than talent. Despite his unassailable patrician credentials, he had found the headwinds stronger at each successive turn of his career. He ran for the consulship and failed twice, a big humiliation in an age when one's honor and prestige were worn on one's sleeve. Catiline determined that only armed revolution would sweep him into power, and so he got to work on a harebrained scheme to overthrow the Roman order and install himself at the top.

The Catiline conspiracy was a sinister plot to murder many prominent people, including the consul Cicero. A renowned orator, Cicero was a contradiction. Despite coming from a humble, provincial background, he quickly rose through the ranks as a defender of conservative prerogative. Touchy about his true place among the senators with ancient familial pedigrees, Cicero, upon hearing about the threat to his life, took the opportunity to cement his credentials by rallying to the defense of the Republic. In a special meeting of the Senate with Catiline in attendance, Cicero revealed the details of the plot to the shocked audience.

One by one, the horrified senators got up and walked away from Catiline, voting with their feet. As Cicero's florid speech progressed, the no-man's-land around the now-disgraced Catiline grew. By the time he was finished, Catiline was left sitting alone with the rest of the Senate standing together on the other side of the meeting house. Catiline was isolated, physically and politically. It didn't take him long to flee the city.

Cicero was lauded as the savior of his country for thwarting the devious scheme, and a vengeful Senate set its will to rooting out any other conspirators. In a matter of weeks, they rounded up a handful of suspected associates. But many in the Senate believed that the conspiracy went even deeper, and rumors circulated about who else might have been plotting revolution. Many cast sideways glances at Caesar. Catiline had run for consul on a populist platform, and Caesar was a populist who was aligned with some of the political reforms that Catiline advocated.

The Senate gathered to debate the fate of the accused, and as praetor-elect for the following year, Caesar was one of the many scheduled to speak. Given the rumors surrounding him, how Caesar acted in these debates would be very closely scrutinized. A few notables spoke before Caesar about how to deal with the conspirators. They were unanimous and emphatic in their cry for immediate and merciless death to all.

Rather than adopt the bloodlust of the senators who spoke before him and cement the fate of the hapless conspirators, Caesar spoke out emphatically *against* execution. He passionately argued in favor of clemency, stating that instead of death, they should be banished to different corners of the empire. They had no more power; they posed no further threat. Caesar was a gifted orator, and his arguments began to weaken the resolve of some in the Senate.

Caesar's speech demonstrated his essential humanity. He could be as ruthless as the next Roman, but he had to be pushed a lot further to take such drastic action. By arguing for banishment, he was arguing for the exercise of power over force. For those paying attention to the happenings in the Senate, Caesar's actions also helped demonstrate that he was a senator, but not *of* the Senate. He was his own man, an independent freethinker who would come to your defense if it was the right thing to do. Caesar stood apart.

Caesar knew what people would say. They would suggest that he had some association with the conspirators and was trying to save them out of a sense of obligation. It didn't matter. He spoke out against the loss of life because it was the right thing to do, even though it would kick the rumor mill into overdrive.

At the conclusion of Caesar's speech, Cicero and Caesar's inveterate foe Cato spoke again. They stiffened the backbone of the Senate and reaffirmed the case for death. The compliant Senate followed their lead, and the conspirators were quickly executed. No trial, no jury, just death. They were strangled by a senatorial executioner that very same day.

Caesar's actions remind us that we are often faced with the choice of doing what we think is right or going with the flow. In the case of the Catiline conspiracy, Caesar genuinely believed that the loss of life, even of those accused of plotting the murder of others, was unnecessary. He spoke up, accepting the fact that people would question his motives for doing so. As Caesar sought to build his power base, he knew the importance of being seen as a person of conviction, someone who could be counted on to be genuine and authentic. He understood that his argument for clemency was as much about gaining future acceptance for his words and actions as it was about saving the lives of the conspirators.

Sometimes following the crowd in the present can give someone reason to doubt you in the future. As unorthodox as Caesar's argument was in the Senate, no one could doubt that it was his own. By defying convention, he helped solidify his reputation as a leader whom the people could trust to speak out against senatorial force. He did what he thought was right, and he turned the situation to his advantage. He showed that he was the kind of leader that the Roman people wanted to follow.

ﻙ

It wasn't just in senatorial proceedings that Caesar established himself as a different kind of patrician. Just when it would seem that this type of behavior could put his life in danger, it ended up helping augment his position and growing his personal legend, as the next story very early on in Caesar's life shows.

It was 75 BC, and young Caesar wasn't behaving the way most captives did. The fierce pirates of the ancient Mediterranean were used to hostages cowering below deck, not calling them "ignorant savages" and demanding quiet so that they could read in peace (and getting away with it). But if Caesar wasn't a typical leader, then he also wasn't a typical hostage.

While still a teenager, Caesar was married off to a young woman whose family had wealth and prestige but deadly political enemies. One of those enemies, Sulla, a ruthless dictator who had been decorating the Forum with the heads of his adversaries, ordered Caesar to divorce his wife in 81 BC. Ever defiant, the young leader refused. Rather than add his head to Sulla's macabre décor, Caesar went on the run, eventually heading east for some well-timed overseas military adventures, winning honors and glory for his bravery.

After Sulla's death in 78 BC, Caesar came back to Rome and took to prosecuting members of the aristocracy for their corrupt fleecing of the poor provincials in Rome's overseas holdings. That the young aristocrat Caesar took up the cause of the poor and dispossessed, defying class conventions and crusading against his own class, was noble indeed. As suspected, the juries acquitted their own, and Caesar realized that he would need more than a just cause to win such cases. His advocacy began to make enough people angry that he decided to head east once again for rhetorical training. He would hone his craft under the masters. Caesar chose the very best. In particular, he sought the same teacher who had helped the great orator and statesman Cicero achieve such lofty heights. After extensive schooling,

Caesar headed back to Rome and in the process was captured by pirates off the coast of Greece, stumbling into a dire threat to his life.

Caesar's captors were delighted to learn of his elite patrician rank and set his ransom at twenty talents of silver (roughly equivalent to seventy pounds today). Caesar was indignant—not at being captured and held hostage, but because he believed that a man of his rank and pedigree should command a much higher ransom. Upon his insistence, his amused captors more than doubled their demands, raising the ransom from twenty to fifty talents of silver. He wanted to be a big deal, and he needed proof that he was seen as such.

As he waited for his family to raise the funds for his release, Caesar settled in to life at sea. But rather than quietly wait in intimidated silence below deck, Caesar readily took to the life of a pirate. He helped on deck and engaged in wrestling matches with his captors. He read speeches to them, and when they didn't like his work, he called them ignorant savages. When he was trying to read below deck and their raucous noise grew to be a distraction, he upbraided them and demanded quiet. He made himself one of them: loud, full of demands, and doing just as he pleased. The pirates took great amusement in this young Roman noble who clearly thought highly of himself. They grew to like him tremendously. They even chortled at Caesar's joking that when he was freed, he would come back and crucify them all.

After a little more than a month at sea, Caesar's family delivered his ransom. He bade his captors good-bye, and one can only imagine that they were disappointed to see him go. Once released, however, Caesar demonstrated that his good-natured joking with the pirates had been deadly serious. He set to work raising a small military force on his own authority.

Caesar found the pirates at their base, and then attacked and captured them. True to his word, he had the pirates crucified, but in what he considered an act of mercy, he had their throats slit to prevent too much suffering. It is the stuff of legend.

Caesar cultivated a view of himself as someone who did things differently, and this created opportunity for him. When kidnapped by pirates, acting differently than your run-of-the-mill hostage created the opportunity for him to enjoy greater freedom of thought and action. It also created the conditions by which he could exact his revenge and restore the stain on his honor. And it certainly didn't hurt Caesar's reputation to have been part of such a larger-than-life adventure!

Any casual student of history can look at Caesar's career and see that it is full of examples of the use of force. In truth, Caesar was no stranger to the use of arms. However, it is important to note how and when he drew the distinction between his use of power and use of force.

When being held captive, Caesar used his power to form friendships with the pirates. His cultivated identity as a man of the people gave him license to move and act more freely than other hostages. But once he was released, Caesar turned to lethal force to grow his reputation.

Caesar had no interest in being a leader to the pirates. He saw them as enemies outside the scope of his leadership. These were the groups that were subject to his ruthless hand, his use of force. Alternatively, he led those within his ranks using his power. In many ways, Caesar blurred the lines more than his contemporaries, granting favors and amnesty to people who should have been his avowed enemies. But even though he was more liberal in his distinctions between "us" and "them," he kept a firm grip on those he considered to be on his team and acted accordingly. Much in the same way, modern leaders must use the boundaries of their organizations as guideposts in choosing between the use of power and the use of force.

DEFY TRADITIONAL DEFINITIONS

Innovation in leadership is as much about framing the problem as it is about seeking solutions and novel approaches. Once we have an image of an idea, concept, or process, it is easy to get trapped in seeing things only in a manner that fits that definition. To give something a name is to be complacent in our understanding of it. Caesar's innovative leadership never fell into this trap. He distilled the issue at hand to its essence in order to see past conventions and definitions. He kept his mind nimble.

Not all of the examples of Caesar's defiance of convention were as colorful as his run-in with the pirates. As entertaining and demonstrative as it was of his going against the grain, it wasn't a supreme test of his leadership. In one such test, about twenty years down the road, Caesar's ability to defy convention and think on his feet turned a potential deadly trap into a decisive advantage.

37

ᴋᵉ

It was 58 BC. Caesar didn't trust his enemy and his enemy didn't trust him. Many times had a commander come to the peace table only to discover that his adversary had lured him into a trap, violating the terms of the parley and ruthlessly dispatching the conned enemy. This scenario was on the minds of both Caesar and his foe, the Germanic commander Ariovistus.

To help each feel secure, they agreed by way of messenger to meet on a hillock in between their respective camps. Only the two commanders and their mounted bodyguards would be present; this would keep each mobile, able to flee quickly in the event of danger. However, this scenario presented Caesar with a problem: He did not have any Roman mounted soldiers in Gaul at his disposal. Caesar's only real cavalry were Gallic allies, and their loyalties were not assured.

If Caesar went at the appointed hour to meet Ariovistus and his Gallic cavalry abandoned him, then he would be alone and at the will of his enemy. If he didn't show up at the peace talk, it would be tough to play the role of the aggrieved party. Besides, honor demanded that Caesar confront his enemy face-to-face. Without trusted cavalry, but needing to maintain his dignity, what was Caesar to do?

Caesar was a master of improvisation. He realized that he didn't need cavalry so much as he needed trusted troops to spend a few minutes on horseback. It didn't matter if these troops were trained in cavalry tactics; what mattered was that Caesar could depend on their loyalty and that he could present a show of force to Ariovistus.

Tapping into his vast reserves of cleverness, Caesar turned to his most trusted unit, the Tenth Legion. He trusted this unit above all others, and they in turn would acknowledge no other commander. Despite their decidedly terrestrial training, Caesar asked the Tenth to mount horses and act the part of cavalry. They happily obliged their commander, and Caesar rode out to his conference. The two sides met, and discussions took place as the commanders sat atop their mounts. Each leader presented his case, but neither saw much merit in what the other had to say. The war was to continue.

It is entirely plausible that many of these soldiers had never even ridden a horse before. And yet, here they were, sitting astride horses arranged for the conference, accompanying their commander to negotiations with a hostile enemy, far away from the safety of their camp. They must have felt like the proverbial fish out of water.

In striking upon this simple solution, Caesar defied orthodoxy. He surveyed the situation and realized that riding experience was not necessary to accomplish the goal that mounted cavalry would have otherwise provided. What he needed most of all was a safety net, and his best and most trusted legion fit the bill. He distilled the situation to its essentials and came up with a novel solution to a quirky but important problem.

For the rest of their history, the unit took on the name Mounted Tenth, carrying forward those few brief moments into their very identity. A Roman legion was ferociously proud and protective of its identity. The fact that they took the name Mounted Tenth shows clearly how important it was for them to be associated with novelty and innovation. They took great pride in being a part of something so far removed from the typical experience of a Roman soldier. Furthermore, honored to be associated with the cleverness of their commander, the Mounted Tenth deepened their loyalty to him. As his career unfolded and the stakes grew larger, the power that this unit gave to Caesar paid massive dividends.

People like to be a part of new and important solutions. A team's morale can surge on the front lines of innovative projects. Challenging conventions, being creative, disrupting the norm—these were just as important to a team's identity then as they are now.

When life is on the line, literally or figuratively, knowing that a leader has invested you with their trust increases your sense of loyalty and obligation toward them. In short, the leader's power grows for having given the trust. This follows a very clear pattern of leadership from Caesar's career that warrants consideration. Time and time again, Caesar found ways to show his organization that he trusted them—as individuals, as units, and as whole armies—and in doing so grew his power.

Power is not binary. Rather, it is a continuum, and the degree of power that someone holds can wax and wane over time. Caesar sought to maintain and increase his power by nurturing, investing in, and growing the connections that he had with people and never took their affections for granted. Caesar is the archetype of the ambitious climber who never lost sight of where he and his power came from.

DEFY ASSUMPTIONS

Part of becoming a dynamic leader is standing out from the rest and getting noticed. But it is not enough to be different for its own sake. Standing out is important, but so is authenticity. Caesar challenged the assumptions that he genuinely felt needed to be challenged. He did not try to take on every single aspect of Roman society, just as a modern leader can't take on every element of a company's culture. We, like Caesar, need to pick our battles.

To stand out as a leader, find the root cause of why things are the way they are and then act accordingly. The first step is to identify the established orthodoxy. Ask yourself: What assumptions are we taking for granted? By mapping out the assumptions that people make, a leader can find the subcurrents running through an organization and find the conventions that need to be defied. Focusing on outdated assumptions that drag down performance or hinder breakthrough ideas is a great place to start.

4

BET ON YOURSELF

M odern leaders often face this dilemma: which of two paths will lead to greater success?

Making tough calls about your career is one of the hardest things a leader has to do. How many times do we find ourselves at a crossroads in our own careers, where competing options or opportunities are so rife with pros and cons that making a decision seems next to impossible? Endless loops of analysis and discussion with close confidants more often than not seem to muddy the waters even further. When you are at a crossroads, which way do you turn?

In the next story, Caesar, nearing the height of his career, met such a crossroads head on. In making his choice, he had to place a bet. He had to bet on himself.

༜

It was 60 BC. For all his cunning, Caesar couldn't be in two places at the same time, and his enemies knew it. Aware of his growing popularity—and power—they sought to stem his rise by any means necessary. They forced him into a choice between two potentially once-in-a-lifetime events: celebrating a triumph and winning the consulship. Standing outside the city, he knew his decision would be critical. Revel in the glory of the people and cement his personal legacy among the greats of Roman history, or chase high office while momentum was on his side?

Caesar had recently completed a governorship in Spain and had achieved more than many thought possible. He had governed wisely and with fairness, settled disputes between antagonists, reorganized finances, and won military victories against those who fought Roman domination. For his smashing victories in the field, his army had hailed him as "imperator," or "commander." This last accomplishment qualified him for the greatest public honor a Roman general could ever hope to attain: the right to celebrate a triumph. At the same time, he was finally eligible to stand for the highest elected office in the land: consul.

For an ambitious leader trying to restore his family's prestige and build his own reputation, the possibility of being awarded the highest military honor and holding the highest elected office in the land was almost too good to be true. The combination of these two, the consulship and celebrating a triumph, would catapult Caesar to new levels of fame and fortune. But always suspicious of people who weren't insiders in their clique, Caesar's enemies in the Senate vowed to prevent this from happening.

Celebrating a triumph was the crowning moment in a military career. The triumphant general, wearing a special gold-embroidered purple toga, would wind his chariot through the streets of Rome, packed with crowds of adoring citizens heaping praise and honor on the conquering hero. The general's chariot would be the focal point in a victory parade that included public displays of the acts of heroism of the commander, the spoils of war, and, when possible, his vanquished enemies in chains. The greater the victory, the greater the display that the hero could put before the citizens of Rome.

From a brand-building perspective, it was tough to beat a triumph. All the residents of Rome would turn out to watch the show. Afterward, the public would join in feasting, usually paid for by the victorious general. Games and theater performances were also staged at various points in the city. From Caesar's point of view, what could be a better tool in gaining the hearts and minds of the Roman citizens and building a power base?

The Romans had extremely long memories, and they judged a contemporary in part by what his ancestors had done, sometimes hundreds of years earlier. A triumph would do great things for Caesar's reputation in the present and the years to come. But so would a consulship. In fact, Romans often referenced events by the names of past consuls—for example, "In the year of Crassus and Pompey." To attain the highest elected office would convey great honor and distinction upon Caesar and his descendants. And given his overwhelming popularity, Caesar was a very strong candidate for the highest office in the land. All he needed to do was present himself in person in Rome to qualify for the upcoming election.

A general anticipating his triumph had to wait outside of the border around Rome, the pomerium, until the day arrived, as it was otherwise against the law to bring armed soldiers in the city. This put Caesar in a difficult situation. If he crossed the border to present himself as a candidate for the consulship, then he would lose his *imperium*, the authority he carried as a commander in the field, and with it the opportunity to celebrate his triumph. However, if he stayed with his army outside the pomerium, he would not be able to qualify as a candidate for the consulship. Noting his dilemma, the Senate, anxious to stem Caesar's rising tide, sprang into action.

For Caesar, there was a simple solution with plenty of historical precedent: candidates had often qualified for office in absentia; all that was required was approval from the Senate for someone to register on his behalf. Caesar had some supporters in the Senate, and on the final day of qualifying, they were prepared to bring forward a request that Caesar be registered as a candidate in absentia. Since there was no legal ground upon which to base an objection and plenty of precedent for such a concession to be granted, the matter should have been open and shut. But the Senate, and the humorless Cato, had other ideas.

Before the measure could be brought to the floor, Cato rose to talk—and talk and talk and talk—preventing any other business from coming up for debate or vote. As the hours passed, it became perfectly clear that Cato was committed to talk until the session expired, meaning that Caesar's allies could not present the petition for him to qualify in absentia. Caesar's petty adversaries were forcing him to choose the path of his career. One can only imagine Cato's smug sense of self-satisfaction.

Word of Cato's move reached Caesar as he hovered with his army on the outskirts of Rome, increasingly anxious as the hours slipped by. It quickly became clear to him that he had to choose between celebrating his triumph and qualifying as a candidate for the consulship.

Caesar was certainly popular, and while he would be a leading candidate for the consulship, there were no guarantees that he would win. Besides, two consuls were elected every year, so if he skipped this election, he could always run one short year later. And with the popularity that would surely follow a triumph, Caesar would be highly likely to gain the office the next time around. Meanwhile, a triumph could be a once-in-a-lifetime opportunity. It was almost without precedent that a general would be awarded a triumph more than once in his career.

On the morning of the following day, Cato and the rest of the Senate awoke to the news that Caesar had slipped into town and presented himself as a candidate for the consulship. He had foregone the triumph, choosing running for the highest office as the most critical thing he could do to advance his career.

To many, this decision seemed strange. Why pass on the unsurpassed glory and prestige of a triumph, something that rarely happened at all, let alone more than once in a career, when the consulship was a prize that could be won every year?

Celebrating personal honor and glory are fine. There is a time and a place for good public relations. Popularity and power often go hand in hand, but they are not the same thing. Caesar understood the distinction and made the choice that would bring him to greater power.

BET ON WHAT MOVES
YOUR MISSION FORWARD

Caesar's goals went beyond his own elevation to high office; he wanted to reform badly outdated elements of Roman society. By choosing a triumph, he would have gained prestige and popularity, and perhaps a degree of power as a by-product. But by standing for the consulship, he could build a platform to drive a transformation agenda. Caesar often cited his own honor as a reason for his actions, but all the honor in the world was meaningless without a way to leverage it for the accomplishment of goals. Caesar bet on himself and his agenda. His choice demonstrated that he was confident that he would earn another triumph at some point down the road. This would prove to be a winning bet, but for now, there was work to be done.

Any leaders seeking to drive change will have their motives questioned. Skeptics, naysayers, and malcontents will seek to undermine leaders pushing for true transformation. Had Caesar waited a year to pursue the consulship, he would have given these people ammunition in the war of words used to derail any change program: "He says these are important changes, yet he put them off a year to pursue his own glory and prestige."

Caesar's actions remind us that when it comes to leadership, the mission comes first, and our own benefits come second. Glory can wait. Critical change cannot. This was certainly a hard choice to make, to put the mission first when it meant turning down the adulation and adoration of the entire Roman citizenry. But people turn to leaders in whom they see authenticity, and Caesar chose the authentic path.

Glory was great, and it mattered deeply to Caesar, but it didn't benefit anyone in his power base to throw a big party. Caesar took his responsibility as a leader seriously, and winning high office was the best thing he could do to help his people make the gains that they so desperately needed. Walking away from a triumph might have meant walking away from love and adulation, but his power base needed him to be their champion, not their hero. A modern leader is no different. If a leader seeks change, then they would do well to follow Caesar's example: put aside the glory and focus on the mission.

If we think about the Roman government as a modern organization, then the Roman system needed serious reforms in terms of governance, workers' rights, transparency, ethics, and the list goes on. The people needed someone who would stand up to senatorial intransigence, someone who would fight for them. Caesar was willing to do so, but he needed the people behind him. As events would prove, having the support of the people was critical to his plans.

As with any modern organization in crisis mode, many people refused to see the challenges as being true threats to the survival of the state. Any leader pursuing a transformation agenda will confront the same challenge. But the broader the base of power, the more stakeholders are available to help pursue the mission. Caesar's actions helped him gain power from those whose support he needed most. A first glance would suggest that Caesar turned down a once-in-a-lifetime opportunity, a triumph, to chase something that was available every year. In fact, Caesar knew that time was of the essence. He made the right choice by betting on himself and his plans for Rome.

BET ON YOUR POWER ROI

Debt is an ever-present aspect of our lives. Many careers begin with financing from student loans. A bet on oneself requires the belief that the investment returns will outpace the cost of debt in the long run. In the story that follows, Caesar's calculation involved what he thought his return on investment would be in terms of power gained.

It was 63 BC. Caesar was in his mid-thirties, and he was running for the exalted and prestigious office of pontifex maximus, or chief priest of the Roman religion. In seeking the office, he was thumbing his nose at Roman tradition. By custom, the position of pontifex maximus was reserved for elderly Roman senators and statesmen, officials with a long and distinguished career of service to the republic. It was not meant for young upstarts still paying their dues and working their way up the ladder of increasingly prestigious offices, and Caesar's candidacy rankled the elite and traditionalists. As he left his family, he announced to them, "I will either return tonight as pontifex maximus, or not at all."

Caesar had bet hugely on himself and taken significant risk in doing so. His opponents in the election were much more traditional candidates, elder statesmen seeking the office as a capstone on long and distinguished careers. It was uncertain if the tradition-obsessed Romans would put someone so young and unproven into the office, regardless of his popularity among the rank-and-file Roman citizens. Caesar knew that if he won the election, his position would be improved. If he lost, however, he would be forced to flee Rome. What could have caused this promising newcomer to be on such shaky ground that exile was the only option following a setback at the polls?

It was more than thumbing his nose at tradition that made Caesar's bet so big: he was under crushing debt. His impoverished childhood meant that he had very little personal resources from which to draw in seeking office. He needed money to finance his ambitions, and he borrowed heavily to do so. His creditors were closing in, and he needed to be elected to office to keep them at bay.

The race for pontifex maximus was not even close: Caesar won handily. He had pushed his personal finances to the breaking point and defied long-standing Roman tradition in order to do it, but he won and took one big step further down the ambitious path that he had laid out for himself. Romans were devout, and getting elected allowed Caesar the opportunity to forge deeper ties with the pious citizenry.

When making big career decisions with financial impact, we can learn from Caesar's example. What are the next-level benefits that a bet-on-self moment can afford? Does it give us better organizational access? Connect us more to the key stakeholders who will help us attain our personal goals? Caesar demonstrated the importance of looking past the simplicity of financial security to the organizational impact of success. He bet on his ability to win, and it paid enormous dividends.

༄

Caesar's biggest bet-on-yourself moment, and one of the most audacious leadership moments of all time, came later on, in 49 BC, when he was faced with a decision that could bring civil war to his beloved Rome.

How could it have come to this? After he had achieved greater military success than any Roman had ever known and become the most beloved person in his country, Caesar's path took a dark turn. To the overwhelming majority of his fellow Romans, he was a hero. To a tiny fraction, he was a villain. In his every action, these people saw their worst fears realized. Thoroughly convinced that Caesar's power was an existential threat, the anti-Caesarians maneuvered the political situation in Rome to bring about his demise. In private discussions and public debates, they worked to undermine and denounce Caesar to all who would listen. The Senate finally passed a decree known as the senatus consultum ultimum, or final act of the Senate. It empowered the consuls and other magistrates to do whatever they deemed necessary to defend the republic. In practical terms, the act achieved two things: it suspended the right of tribunes to veto senatorial decrees, and it declared Caesar an enemy of the state.

For good reason, Caesar's allies feared for their safety. Those that were tribunes knew that their office no longer held any political advantage—without the power of the veto, they had no way to check senatorial aggression. They decided to flee to Caesar, smuggling themselves out of Rome in a rented cart, and making straight for their comrade. The use of force to assert political will, the old senatorial way of leading, loomed in the air.

In the preceding hours, Caesar had made a show of going about his business in the usual way, bathing and dining casually, and conspicuously. As evening became night, Caesar rode off, parting ways with his closest companions. Nothing seemed amiss, and no one noticed as Caesar doubled back and regrouped with his comrades in the dark of night, meeting up at the river Rubicon.

The small river was raging with waters from heavy rains, perhaps a harbinger of what was to come. While there was little about the river itself that was noteworthy, it had the important distinction of being the boundary between the provinces on one side and the Italian mainland, the home turf of the Romans, on the other. One side was foreign territory, the other home.

Caesar stared into space and considered his choices: invade Roman territory and plunge the known world into civil war; or give up his command, return to Rome, and allow his enemies to pursue their vendetta in the courts. In his lifetime, Caesar had seen the devastating effects of civil war: bloodshed, terror, and families being torn apart. He himself had spent terror-filled months as a youth, fleeing from bounty hunters seeking to collect the prize on his head set for defying an order to divorce his young wife.

Eventually, he was removed from the list of state-sponsored targets, but the memory of being young and on the run stuck with him.

Accustomed to leading armies of tens of thousands, Caesar had but one legion at his side now, a few thousand foot soldiers and a couple of hundred cavalry waiting for his orders. One can only imagine the many dark thoughts swirling around in Caesar's head as he stared blankly across the swift-moving river, his comrades waiting for his decision. At last, he said, "The die is cast." He had made his choice, and by morning the rest of the Roman world would know which path he had followed.

Despite the gravity of the decision he faced, there is nothing to suggest that Caesar ever looked back or questioned his judgment. His followers never had any doubt in his ability to make the right decision. They took great comfort in following a leader who did not second-guess himself at the first sign of hardship. Caesar's tone as a leader was that his path was the straight and true path, and his followers believed in him unconditionally.

"The die is cast," Caesar said as he made his decision. He crossed the Rubicon and invaded his home territory.

Caesar had spent his entire career defying tradition, eschewing force and cultivating power through influence. Had he failed? Had his leadership style been unsuccessful? I don't believe so. Caesar didn't seek civil war; in many ways, civil war came to him. He desperately sought to broker compromises in the lead-up to the invasion. He sought peace and practically begged those back in Rome to find a better way forward. They ignored him over and over, either failing to respond or doing so with outlandish and completely untenable demands. And even now, if force was the only course of action he could take, he was going to do it his own way—out and in front of the situation.

Caesar had a style all his own, and nothing about the war at hand was going to change things. His conflict was with Cato, Pompey, and the Senate, not the Roman people. Amazingly, he made his invasion with one legion, only about 10 percent of his fighting strength. If ever there was a bet-on-yourself moment for Caesar, this was it.

What could have been seen as reckless was a truly astonishing act of self-confidence. When facing decisions of great gravity and engaging in a big battle—whether literally or metaphorically—many times we wait and wait until we have every possible bit of our fighting strength at the ready. Marshaling resources takes time and allows others to get their ducks in a row as well. On the other hand, acting quickly forces others to react, and seizing the initiative in complex and tense moments carries enormous benefit. When faced with the biggest decision of his career, Caesar bet on his abilities, despite his vastly diminished fighting strength. He deemed his own abilities as a leader to be his most crucial asset.

It is worth reflecting on Caesar's leadership position at this point. Whom exactly was Caesar trying to lead? His army, always the center of his authority and the source of much of his power, was certainly part of his organization. But Caesar was a genuine reformer, and the Roman system was broken in many ways. He had succeeded in delivering reforms where others had died trying, by keeping focused on his definition of his organization: the Roman people themselves. Caesar learned from an early age that the people at the bottom have more combined influence than those who lead them. In the common Romans, he found the base from which he would build his power. He trusted them to be his people, and in turn they trusted him to be their champion.

Most careers have humble origins. No matter what advantages we call upon to start our climb up the ladder, rarely do we start at the top rung. Caesar certainly didn't. He had been born into a family with impeccable patrician credentials, but what his family had in prestige, it lacked in resources. Despite his noble pedigree, Caesar grew up among the destitute, downtrodden, and disenfranchised. It was this experience that allowed him to build an authentic image of himself as a man of the people.

Caesar was constantly sizing up the nature of the organization that he was trying to lead. In his example we find an important modern parallel. Defining the scope of our leadership ambitions can be an extremely useful filter in guiding our course of actions. Often, ambitious people want to be seen as leaders by everyone they come across. This can dilute action and cloud judgment in critical situations. A sober assessment of exactly whom a leader is trying to lead and why can help drive better decisions.

BET ON YOUR PEOPLE TO BET ON YOU

With such a limited force, Caesar needed every soldier he had. However, he was not interested in making people fight against their conscience. He allowed any soldier who chose to do so to leave unharmed with all their possessions. This simple yet extraordinary act garnered the respect and loyalty of his army.

Caesar did not demand that everyone in his organization see things his way. As a leader, he gave people space to draw their own conclusions and make their own bets. As a result, when they followed him, they were doing so from a place of authenticity. When people feel that they are part of a decision-making process, they are much more inclined to take ownership of actions and outcomes. Caesar's opt-in policy at the Rubicon only deepened his organization's commitment to follow him from that point forward.

Allowing rank-and-file soldiers to opt out was one thing, but giving senior officers the same leeway was another. And yet, Caesar took the same approach even when one of his top generals refused to participate in the campaign. Unwilling to take the next step of open rebellion, one of Caesar's most capable and longest-serving lieutenants, Labienus, left the army. A typical Roman general would have treated the defection as treason and sent a force to follow and kill the subordinate. Caesar took a different path, having all of Labienus's baggage and personal effects gathered and sent to him.

Engaged in the opening of a civil war and wrapped in the cloak of self-righteousness, Caesar had the foresight and intellectual discipline to stop and consider that everyone might not want to follow this course of action. What's more, he went the next step and considered what to do about it. Should he ignore the issue, hoping that the men would remain silent in their opposition? Should he forcefully root out all opposition, purging his own ranks before even getting started and thus creating an atmosphere of distrust and contempt? Again, Caesar's remarkable insight into the human psyche illuminates our own leadership path. A leader can't stop and give people an opt-out at every turn, but at this critical juncture, Caesar made sure that he was putting his life and career on the line only with people who were truly committed, with those who bet on him.

Caesar didn't pretend that everyone in the organization was on board, and he didn't fool himself into thinking that everyone should be, either. Part of betting on himself meant having thick skin and being OK with dissent. As always, he sought to lead only those who were willing to be led. Sometimes he used charm to win people over. But rarely, if ever, did he physically punish someone or seek retribution when they didn't come around to his way of thinking. Betting on himself meant using power, not force. He knew that force only marginalizes power and that someone forced to stay would only foster discontent.

True leadership flows out of true confidence. Forgoing the glory of a triumph to stand for election, leveraging debt to finance his career, and crossing the Rubicon—in each case, Caesar parlayed his self-confidence into stronger organizational faith in his abilities and commitment to his cause. If we cannot take firm action and have the courage of our conviction, then how can anyone inside our organization be expected to do the same?

The civil war that followed the crossing of the Rubicon defined Caesar's career and, in many ways, his legacy. Even in a literal life-and-death struggle, he sought to unlock people's intrinsic motivation. By betting on himself and following the playbook of power over force, Caesar accomplished more than anyone could have predicted.

There are certain decisions one has to make that seem difficult at the time, but once they are made, they are obvious in retrospect. In many cases, this is because we failed in the decision-making process to evaluate and consider the second- and third-level benefits that would come from making these decisions.

Our natural, hard-wired tendency toward loss aversion often makes the cons loom larger than the pros in our minds. Caesar demonstrated a much subtler and nuanced grasp of risk and reward; he was able to look past the immediate consequences of bold career moves and to the bigger picture. By looking at the path of his career, we understand the importance of seeing beyond the immediate implications of an action to its next-level benefits. For Caesar, the return on investment for his risky choices was a deeper level of access to the people whose support he would need to achieve his ambitious agenda. He knew instinctively that the path to great leadership involved not getting caught up in fleeting rewards.

֍

Caesar's insight was that the best risks were ones that were taken when he could control the outcome through his own talent and ambition, and resulted in an increase in his most treasured asset: power.

5

KEEP THE LINES OF COMMUNICATION OPEN

Most organizations have experienced failed change management efforts. In many cases, the cause of the failure was not the strategy, but rather the cultural acceptance of the change itself. Convinced of the rightness and necessity of transformation, leaders often overlook the fact that other key people may take longer to develop the same point of view.

Having a lofty title doesn't guarantee a license to operate, in and of itself. People may be respectful of a senior position but are not often awed by it. Therefore, understanding power dynamics and whose opinions matter is an important exercise for any leader. Caesar was a master at navigating power dynamics and finding the right ways to get the right people on board with his plans. As the next story shows, his skills as a communicator and connector were key to motivating his power base and furthering his reform agenda for Rome.

It was 60 BC. Politics in the late Roman Republic was a maelstrom of shifting alliances, family vendettas, and social disharmony. Caesar had run for the consulship, the highest office in the land, and when the votes were cast, he came out on top by a wide margin.

Winning the position garnered prestige for himself and his family, access to a platform for reforming a dying political system, and the opportunity for lasting military glory as a governor after his term of office ended. In large part, Caesar was seeking to bring forward his family's legacy from the past to the present. But being consul was not itself a guarantee of long-term success. What is true today was just as true two thousand years ago: every step up the ladder means that the winds of resistance grow stronger.

While in office, elected officials could not be charged with crimes, real or imagined. But once out of office, anything was fair game, including trumped-up charges engineered to take down an opponent or unwind any of his previous victories. Countless magistrates had seen their terms of office end with immediate prosecution for their actions. Many ended up in exile. In Caesar's case, his political enemies had resolved to see him end in failure, either by stopping his election, defeating his agenda during his consulship, or unwinding his program afterward.

Personal rivalry can fester over time. When things are going well, the consequences of such dynamics are an annoyance. In times of crisis, fear and suspicion replace trust and collaboration, and dysfunction becomes increasingly pervasive. The political atmosphere in Rome at the time of Caesar's ascension to the consulship was fetid. Discord was the order of the day. As Rome had grown increasingly prosperous, the poor and dispossessed flocked to the city seeking relief. Along with the growing masses of the downtrodden, many of Pompey's troops were returning home to find themselves homeless and destitute.

Caesar had planned his goals long before gaining the office. He genuinely cared about the well-being of ordinary Romans, and he sought to be a strong voice for them in a system that ignored them. Empathy was a cornerstone of his policies. Caesar's populism wasn't a tactic to curry favor for votes. Such a ploy would have had little lasting effect. Unlocking support has to be based on genuine value exchange.

Caesar knew that to deepen the ties that he had forged with the people, he would have to bring something substantive to the table and do so from a place of authenticity. But he had a stark reality to confront as he prepared for his consulship. He might have won election to the highest political office in the land, but he was far from Rome's leading man. He couldn't simply snap his fingers and push his legislative program into place. It would take considerable skill to gain any measure of success. And so he got to work long before his term of office began.

A frequent and consummate communicator, Caesar sent letters and messengers to leading senators and influencers. He sought to pre-sell his ambitious legislative agenda and flush out the obstacles he would encounter upon its introduction. His soft-sell approach let him know what changes and modifications needed to be made to work around senatorial intransigence. He carefully laid the groundwork to pre-empt objections and gain support where he could.

COMMUNICATE WITH YOUR
FOLLOWERS *AND* RESISTORS

Upon entering office, Caesar had already done an extraordinary amount of work to progress his plans for Rome. Before taking office, he had mapped out all of the people who would be critical stakeholders to the success of his agenda and carefully cultivated communication with them. Writing letters, making visits, and sending representatives on his behalf, Caesar knew that framing expectations and engaging key stakeholders would increase the probability of success for his aggressive agenda. As events unfolded, his communications yielded enormous benefit in terms of direct impact, but more important, they revealed the fact that his opposition was acting in bad faith.

Caesar's major goal as consul was one that had led to the demise of many change agents before him: land reform. He understood the magnitude of his task—it was a life-or-death proposition. Before he pushed his agenda forward, he gave people a chance to absorb and react. He needed to get people on board, not only for the sake of the legislation but also for his own health and safety. Resistance was guaranteed to be heavy, and he needed to make inroads against it. Power was key. If he could get people to want to follow, then he might have a chance. And if he couldn't, then he could at least hope to soften their resistance.

Caesar knew that part of taking on ambitious change is keeping the lines of communication open—even with the resistors. People are more likely to get behind an agenda if they feel that they've had a chance to weigh in. Caesar sought to create the conditions under which even the naysayers could feel comfortable about getting with his program. Yes, the situation was critical and reform was urgently needed. But Caesar took his time engaging his stakeholders to prime the pump for success.

Caesar shows us the importance of inviting the feedback of people from whom we may expect resistance. It is so easy to ignore or turn a deaf ear toward those we suspect are against our plans, especially when, with the near ubiquity of mass media and the proliferation of communication tools today, it's easier than ever to find people who already agree with us. Inviting dialogue creates the conditions under which naysayers can be identified and, ideally, won over. At the very least, it is an opportunity to dampen the extent of their resistance.

Caesar's modus operandi was to "move people up a level": neutralize vocal critics, turn neutrals into supporters, and turn supporters into advocates and proselytizers. Wherever people fell on this continuum, Caesar engaged with them with the goal of advancing his relationship. He was pragmatic enough to know that not everyone could be won over. For these people, lessening their resistance was a victory. No one should be overlooked.

In this demonstration of power over force, Caesar shows us that power creates options. There are many levels of support, and it is worthwhile to try to move a stakeholder up a level. Conversely, force is polarizing: "You're either with me or against me." There is less room for empathy and more room for enmity. Caesar's pre-selling of his legislative agenda, and his lifelong commitment to open and frank communications with all, offered limitless permutations of mutual value exchange. Through these actions, he enhanced people's desire to follow. They were more vested in outputs for having participated in the inputs.

When the time came for Caesar to make his big push for reform, more people were willing to support him and fewer sought to oppose him. He had grown his power base. For Caesar, power and communication went hand in hand; the act of communicating openly was key to cultivating power.

COMMUNICATE SO THAT THEY HEAR

Upper echelons of management and upper echelons of politics have this in common: They both use special "in-the-know" jargon to justify and protect their exalted positions. Fancy words, turns of phrases, and acronyms are often deployed as a buffer between their lofty heights and the rest of the organization. Think of how different the language in the boardroom is from the language in the cafeteria. Jargon is a special tool designed to insulate the bigwigs from the rank and file. Caesar avoided this trap. He didn't speak to impress or to demonstrate status and rank. On the contrary, he spoke to connect, to be understood, and to be a uniquely identifiable voice. Caesar spoke to be heard.

We will explore Caesar's deft management of his tumultuous year as consul in the next chapter. But for now, let's skip ahead to the chaotic period that followed his consulship.

🖉

It was 58 BC. Per Roman custom, upon the end of their term in office, consuls were sent to the provinces to act as governors in what was called the proconsulship. These terms were usually set at one year. Caesar's term stretched to ten. Early in his proconsulship, Caesar faced an unexpected challenge. He knew that while he was far removed from the political action in the heart of Rome, his adversaries would work to erode his base of power, chipping away at his assets and marginalizing him whenever possible.

He had taken great care to leave allies safely in important elected offices to look after his interests. Confederates could buffer senatorial aggression, but this left him with one big problem unaccounted for: how to maintain his greatest source of power, the relationship he had so carefully forged with the everyday citizens of Rome. It had taken him his whole career to establish himself as their champion. A decade was a long time to spend away from a group of people whose love and affection mattered so deeply to his career. Caesar risked having his power base atrophy due to neglect.

Communication, it seemed, was the key. As he moved through his proconsulship, Caesar began documenting his actions. He dispatched back to Rome the *Commentaries*, his firsthand account (told in the third person) of the actions and situations facing him and his army. These documents, which survive largely intact and offer wonderful perspectives on Caesar and his times, served a very important purpose for the leader. They gave him the opportunity to control, or at least influence, the narrative surrounding key events. It might be a bit glib to call the *Commentaries* propaganda, but his writings definitely helped him to maintain control of how his actions were interpreted back in the capital.

Caesar's writing was masterful—but in plain and direct prose. It is clear that his intended audience was not the upper echelons of the Roman elite but the average citizens who made up the majority of his power base. By communicating directly with the people, often from the front lines of critical battlefields, Caesar nurtured his special relationship with them. He invited them into his world to see what he saw, to face the same obstacles he faced, and to understand his thought process.

Caesar's writings were an investment in keeping his followers loyal as well as in burnishing his reputation. The language of the *Commentaries* is important when considering their true aim. There were no lofty rhetorical flourishes or words designed to obfuscate meaning. Caesar wrote to be understood by as many people as possible.

Paradoxically, modern mass communications and technology make it easier to overlook the necessity of organization-wide communications. With so much one-on-one back-and-forth between individuals, taking the time to update an entire team on what's happening is a critical but often overlooked leadership tool. Often we assume that a few well-timed emails will make their way around to the rest of the team.

One of the reasons Caesar avoided specialty jargon was because he wanted his message to be broadly disseminated.

Using plain, accessible language, he kept a direct line of communication between himself and the people of Rome. As a result, they grew closer to him, even while he was far away. And when Caesar's detractors sought to undermine his popularity, they found themselves confronting a public that had heard Caesar's point of view directly.

A leader who can make everyone in his or her organization feel exalted and empowered will gain tremendously in terms of support and loyalty. A hallmark of Caesar's leadership approach was to make people feel elevated to his level, above the status that Roman society would have otherwise assigned them. For Caesar, such efforts yielded enormous dividends. In his career-long goal of building and growing a power base, his on-the-level communications with the people of Rome made them feel a part of his accomplishments, making his cause their cause.

COMMUNICATE A SINGULAR FOCUS

At moments of great tension and consequence, an organization does well with extraordinary focus. It is wonderful when members of the team find common cause and develop relationships with one another. But if those groups are not aligned to an organizational mission, then unified action is difficult to rally in critical times. The survival of an organization depends on the alignment of goals, something Caesar reinforced repeatedly.

He did what others would consider impossible, in large measure because of the shared purpose of his team. It helped him to build an empire, as the next story shows, and it can help us modern leaders too.

🖎

As Caesar's Gallic campaigns reached their zenith, a visionary and charismatic chieftain named Vercingetorix rallied the various Gallic tribes under a common banner, uniting them in the shared cause of eliminating the Roman menace. The uprising swept across Gaul while Caesar frantically sought to stamp out their resistance.

Over time, the superior discipline, unity, and logistics of the Roman army wore down the Gauls, and Vercingetorix led his army in retreat to the hill town of Alesia. Caesar quickly built a wall of fortifications to trap Vercingetorix and his army by laying siege and being patient. He was betting on winning not by the sword but through the stomach (i.e., starving them into submission).

Trapped and with diminishing options, the Gallic rebels sneaked out word of their plight. In short order, another army was raised—tens of thousands strong—and they began their march to Alesia to relieve the besieged Vercingetorix. Now Caesar faced the possibility of an attacking army with a wall at his rear. He and his team could get trapped against the very fortifications they had built for the siege. He called a council of war and sought the opinions of his lieutenants. Should they flee in advance of the massive army and their suddenly tenuous position? Or should they try to hold out for victory while their deadly adversary was within grasp?

Caesar opened up dialogue, valuing the input and ideas of his subordinates. But even though he held frequent councils of war, using the ideas and experiences of those around him to help work toward better decisions, he remained the sole decision maker. He took ownership of his decisions and full responsibility for their outcomes. He never assigned blame for defeats.

It is easy to give in to temptation and assign blame for our own poor decisions. This might make us feel better in the short term, but the long-term disadvantages of doing so can be severe. Team dynamics are critical to bringing an organization forward, and undermining the trust that team members have in their leader and with one another is dangerous. A team that has the support and loyalty of their leader is a team that will offer better inputs and perspectives. By being the sole owner of critical decisions, Caesar removed any fear from his subordinates that if their advice or input led to unfavorable outcomes, he would punish them. Since there was no blowback for speaking their mind, they were bolder in offering their opinions, and the advice that Caesar received was better.

With an army on either side of his troops, and with the input of his subordinates, Caesar resolved himself to a course of action and acted quickly and decisively. He had already built a set of fortifications to trap Vercingetorix inside Alesia. He knew that the key to ending the Gallic rebellion was to capture the one leader who had managed to unite the fragmented tribes and organize a cohesive resistance. Fleeing was not an option; but then again, getting trapped and smashed by the relief army was certainly not a great option, either.

Caesar's solution was a massive gamble, one that lives on as one of the most audacious battlefield tactics ever conceived.

Doubling down on his position, Caesar ordered a second set of fortifications built farther out, a defensive wall between his army and the relief army marching to Vercingetorix's aid. He put his army between the two walls, one to keep the relief army out, and one to keep Vercingetorix in. Caesar committed his men to victory: either they would take Alesia and capture the rebel leader, or they would be smashed between the two armies, trapped on both sides by the very walls they had built, instruments of their own destruction.

Part of Caesar's army held the outer wall, fending off the relief army and defending their fortifications. The other force broke into Alesia, routing the Gauls and tracking down the rebel commander. Vercingetorix was taken prisoner, and once the rebel king was in Roman hands, the Gallic rebellion evaporated. As the din of the campaign settled down, the weight of Caesar's accomplishment came into focus.

Caesar's brazen act of trapping his army between two walls had the effect of giving his army great purpose. It became fight or die. Working together on a common goal was, literally, a life-or-death proposition.

Furthermore, setting a near-impossible goal for his army was in part what led them to do the extraordinary: fend off one army and defeat another at the same time. Caesar knew that the esprit de corps depended on a sense of being a part of something bigger—in this case, making history. The simple act of trapping his army between two walls took on deeper significance, and the army responded with vigor. Caesar understood the importance of big, bold undertakings as a galvanizing force for the brand and mystique of a leader. People are more likely to follow someone who thinks they can do the impossible.

COMMUNICATE YOUR SUCCESSES

Direct, accessible, and frequent communications to the organization can and should be a part of a leader's arsenal. In addition to gaining their respect and loyalty, leaving a record of key events and decisions provides a leader with an enduring imprint, a legacy.

Caesar's success established Rome as a true pan-European empire. Books have been written about this period of Caesar's career. His goals were ambitious beyond description, and the impacts of his campaigns are felt to this day. For Caesar, legacy and reputation were critical in the years that followed his consulship, as this next story shows.

*

Over the years of campaigning, Caesar took his army to greater and greater heights. Building on the idea that his leadership could take Romans anywhere, Caesar sailed over the edge of the world. The foggy island of Britain had been known for some time, but the island itself was thought to be the end of the world. Getting to this land, shrouded in mystery, seemed an impossible and dangerous undertaking. But Caesar knew that Romans valued courage and conquest, and going to Britain offered both.

Starting in 55 BC, and over the course of a year, Caesar led two invasions into Britain. Despite being of questionable military value, they were a massive boost to his legacy. If he could lead people to the edge of the earth, then there was nothing he couldn't do as a leader. His legend was cemented. His reports from Britain whipped the citizens back in Rome into a frenzy of excitement. The Roman standard had been planted at the very edge of the known world, and Caesar had made it happen. His leadership swelled the Roman pride and sense of exceptionalism.

There is an apparent contradiction at the heart of communications. Leaders should project humility, but the very act of communicating accomplishments seems to contradict this goal. In the example of Caesar, however, we find the necessity of overcoming this hesitancy. Communications, frequent and substantive, bring stakeholders into a leader's decisions and help develop mutual understanding. Additionally, by keeping a dialogue open with various groups and individuals, a leader can spot emergent troubles sooner and take steps to rectify them. All throughout his life and career, Caesar set the example by which modern leaders can connect with friend and foe alike, and take an organization to ever greater heights.

6

CO-OPT THE POWER
OF OTHERS

Think of how often we see political infighting within an organization. Many times, people are asked to choose sides, and it becomes a battle of "You're either with me or against me." Careers and livelihoods fall victim to disagreements carried on between big personalities elsewhere in the organization. Those who straddle the line of neutrality can barely avoid getting swept up in the shifting tides. Sometimes, people just don't have a side in a fight, and forcing an either/or choice alienates these poor souls who would have been useful regardless of the outcome.

In Caesar's campaigns during the early days of the civil war, we see the benefit of a much more gracious and productive way of dealing with competing interests.

In chapter 4, we explored how Caesar bet on himself, making the decision to cross the Rubicon and bringing the awful possibility of a Roman civil war to reality (49 BC). Here is more of that story.

🌿

Normally, an invading army created a wake of destruction and bloodshed. The loot it acquired was considered to be one of the prime motivators for fighting. "Win and get rich" was a pretty simple manifesto. Besides, sacking one city sent an example to the others. But as Caesar advanced toward Rome, he and his army showed great courtesy toward the Italian cities they crossed. He wanted no ordinary Romans to come to harm. Caesar's attitude was, "If you're not against me, then you're with me." This more tolerant approach often softened the path in front of his army.

About a month into the campaign, Caesar encountered his first serious resistance. The town of Corfinium was under the command of the ardent anti-Caesarian, Ahenobarbus (the great-great-grandfather of the future Emperor Nero). Ahenobarbus had once run for consul on a platform of recalling Caesar from his command. For nearly a decade, he had joined with Cato to fight, stall, and undermine Caesar at every turn. Now, as Caesar approached, Ahenobarbus dug in, determined to resist.

Caesar's army had grown considerably, and it prepared to lay siege to Corfinium. Ahenobarbus was counting on senatorial commanders to send reinforcements, but they deemed the city to be indefensible and sent word that no troops would be coming. Ahenobarbus told his men that help was on its way but secretly made plans to escape. When word of his betrayal leaked, his men mutinied, arresting their commander and sending word to Caesar that they were surrendering. Most of these troops changed sides, declaring their loyalty to Caesar. Not only had Caesar won a great victory, but also he had grown substantially stronger while getting his hands on one of the ringleaders of the enemy, all without the loss of life.

With one of his bitterest enemies now his captive, Caesar shocked everyone around him, most especially Ahenobarbus:

he pardoned this great adversary. Ahenobarbus had been one of the leading belligerents in the Senate for years. Full of blister, vitriol, and rhetoric, he had been among the most vocal calling for Caesar's recall and prosecution. And Caesar let him go, unharmed. It was a remarkable act of clemency. This simple act has come down through history as one of Caesar's greatest leadership moments.

Caesar's clemency toward Ahenobarbus was part of a general policy of civility and leniency that was a hallmark of Caesar's leadership. Forgiveness, he felt, would dampen future resistance by planting a seed of doubt in the minds of those who might stand in his way. His enemies claimed that he was a tyrant, that if he were allowed to maintain power, he would unleash bloodshed and terror. Caesar proved them wrong, undermining the way that his opponents sought to undermine him. His clemency was also a subtle invocation of power: only Caesar could grant a pardon. By using his power for good, he not only asserted his position but co-opted the power of Ahenobarbus. He softened the view of Ahenobarbus's followers toward him with this act of benevolence.

Caesar understood that those committed to resistance are going to resist. For these people, dangling a grim punishment over their heads will just make their resistance more spirited, and a policy of revenge will only make things worse. The same applies to organizational politics. Caesar was able to see past his ego and let go of the impulse toward revenge. Little would be accomplished by starting cycles of recrimination, and much was to be gained by showing mercy.

Caesar's clemency was not purely altruistic. There was an important and somewhat subversive element to this policy, which still holds today. By forgoing the socially acceptable process of revenge, Cacsar swung people into his debt. They owed him. The case of Ahenobarbus is one of the starkest examples, but Caesar's career contains countless examples of his clemency. Not only did he let his enemies go free unharmed, but also he welcomed them into his trust, bestowing upon them offices and honors. Over the course of his career, these personal debts accrued and became critical to growing Caesar's power base.

Through his policy of clemency, Caesar lowered the upfront resistance he faced, softened the battles fought, and accrued political capital. Most important, he took a good portion of the power away from the recipients of his clemency for himself. They now had incentive to follow him: they owed their life to him. Consider the anecdote at the beginning of this book, where we see Caesar quash a potentially devastating rebellion by letting his troops know that they had deeply wronged him and then offering them his forgiveness.

No such magnanimity would be extended if people crossed Caesar a second time, however. They had proved that they lacked loyalty and had exhausted their political usefulness, the attributes that Caesar valued and sought the most. If power is the ability to influence and compel intrinsic action, then multiple instances of defiance and resistance proved that he had no power over them. When confronted with these rare occurrences, Caesar generally showed little mercy.

CO-OPT THE POWER OF THE LESS POWERFUL WITH KINDNESS

Kindness, grace, and diplomacy are strong competitive weapons. They can undermine the fighting spirit of the competition and create goodwill. In an age when talent is scarce and good people are often free agents, the way an organization treats its own people as well as its competitors can give it power. In the story that follows, Caesar's reaction to finding enemies in his own camp illustrates how our own teams should interact with the competition.

With the surrender of Corfinium, the path to Rome lay open. Caesar's respect for the lives and property of the citizens whose cities he invaded had caused resistance to evaporate, and he was able to move much more quickly than his opposition could handle. As the civil war progressed, Caesar's policy of clemency continued to build and consolidate his power.

After his campaign in Italy, Caesar quickly turned to Spain to contend with the forces deployed by Pompey, his chief rival in the civil war. In Spain, families, friends, and neighbors found themselves staring across enemy lines at each other. They had reluctantly been brought into conflict through the chasm of civil war. With armies in close contact, soldiers on both sides eventually began fraternizing, roaming freely about the camps of their enemies. Sensing an opportunity to score a quick if largely insignificant victory, the Pompeian commander personally led a murderous rampage, slaughtering Caesarians within his camp.

Some were killed, some hid, and others escaped. Caesar, never one to miss an opportunity to demonstrate his magnanimity, allowed the Pompeians in his camp to leave peacefully or, should they so choose, join his army. He saw that he had nothing to gain by putting the enemies in his camp to the sword. What was a handful of fewer soldiers against the whole balance of an army? And by offering clemency and kindness toward the enemy, he built his legacy as a moderate and fair-minded leader.

Caesar courted a peaceful settlement, pointing out that fighting battles needlessly wasted Roman lives. He took great effort to blur the lines between "his" organization and "theirs." His policy of kindness toward the enemy won him substantially more than it had risked. The fighting spirit of his army swelled while that of his enemy teetered on collapse. Unable to hold their position, the Pompeian generals surrendered Spain, which had been considered a stronghold of Pompey. Through their rash use of force, Pompey's generals had greatly undermined their own cause. In contrast, Caesar used his power to neutralize a big chunk of resistance and lost only seventy men in the process. The campaign began with the armies roughly even in strength. In a short period of time, the fighting spirit of his enemies evaporated. He achieved victory when they acknowledged his supremacy and came to him en masse, truly a triumph of power over force.

The success of Caesar's actions is a poignant reminder of the importance of graciousness toward those around you, especially those you are trying to win over. Caesar cleverly co-opted the power of his adversaries. The enemy factions at Corfinium and in Spain surrendered to him, almost en masse, and almost entirely without bloodshed. Through the use of pardons and fair-mindedness, Caesar won greater loyalty from more people and created a huge sense of obligation to him.

CO-OPT THE POWER OF THE MORE POWERFUL THROUGH COLLABORATION

Power is centered on the individual. But through alliances, the power of others can be co-opted. A leader can extend their own power and influence through the relationships they forge with other key stakeholders. By aligning goals and values, and bringing legitimate value to the table, even junior partners in formal or informal alliances can grow their power through associations.

Throughout Caesar's career he leveraged his skills as a conciliator to co-opt the power of others to his own advantage. In fact, in this strategy lies what was his political masterstroke.

🖝

Rome was crazy about history and tradition. At the time he was elected consul (59 BC), Caesar was on the rise, perhaps on his way to a potentially great career. However, he did not possess much of a history of accomplishments from which to draw. Despite his election to the consulship, he was contending with far more prominent people who had their own pressing agendas. He came into office as a small part of a big system, and with plenty of former consuls, distinguished citizens, and conquering generals floating around, the waters were murky as to where power truly lay. His predecessors all felt entitled to put forth their opinions; what is more, they had the authority of their history to back them up. Meanwhile, Caesar was an outsider and a populist. The conservative Senate distrusted him, and to top it all off, his co-consul for the year, Bibulus, absolutely hated him.

When Caesar took office, the two most prominent Romans were Crassus and Pompey. They were exceedingly powerful in the way that Caesar strived so ardently to be, and each had his own agenda and massive resources on which to draw. However, they were quite jealous of one another, and as a result, neither had been able to realize his goals, and both had grown increasingly frustrated at their futility. Enter the upstart Caesar. The consulship gave him the perfect opportunity and platform to do what no one else could: mediate between Crassus and Pompey.

Caesar organized an agreement between the three to support each other's causes: Crassus would get financial relief for the struggling corporations in which he'd invested, Pompey would get land for his soldiers and validation for his eastern campaign, and Caesar would have help advancing his forthcoming land reform bill. This land reform issue, so important to the fate of the crumbling republic, had led to the downfall and death of many before him, and Caesar needed every bit of political firepower he could get his hands on in the looming fight with the belligerent oligarchs in the Senate.

This three-way alliance came to be known as the First Triumvirate. History has come to view the First Triumvirate as three powerbrokers working in concert for their respective aims. When we look deeper, we discover that the catalyst for this arrangement was the rivalry between the two great men, Crassus and Pompey. In a way, it was the power of the other that stopped both of them from getting what they wanted. Their rivalry helped create divisiveness in the Roman system, which in turn slowed down each man's agenda. By indulging in petty infighting, Crassus and Pompey played right into the hands of the Senate, which had a vested interest in keeping the two in an antagonistic position lest anyone become too powerful on his own.

Caesar brought two powerful rivals together, reaping extraordinary personal gain. His agenda wasn't limited to getting his policies advanced; he wanted to elevate himself through association. It should not be overlooked that he was the least powerful and accomplished of the three—by a wide margin. Caesar gained power by partnering with the most powerful people in Rome. Looking inside our own organizations for similar opportunities can yield great benefit. Conflict can often be destructive—especially in light of mutually beneficial alternatives. Powerful be the peacemakers.

Given their stature and resources, why did Crassus and Pompey need Caesar in the first place? The truth is, they probably didn't—if only they could put aside their enmity to work together. Alas, they couldn't, and Caesar immediately recognized the opportunity presented by their rivalry.

Take note of this important qualifier, however: a junior partner cannot simply hang around senior leaders with political influence and expect to benefit from their greatness without offering anything in return. Leaders seeking to advance or secure their positions should carefully consider the need for reciprocity. In this case, Caesar brought a few very valuable assets to the partnership. For one, his office served as a platform from which he could pursue the agendas of his partners. For another, he brought the skill of mediation. Neither Crassus nor Pompey benefited from their rivalry, and Caesar showed them how they could benefit by working together.

Caesar managed to persuade Crassus and Pompey to put aside their mutual dislike and work as a team. By combining their power, they all stood to gain in a way that they could not on their own. Now, Caesar approached something akin to equal footing. Creating a sense of debt and obligation is also quite useful in the development of individual power. He did not have the prestige and martial accomplishments of Pompey. He did not have the limitless financial resources of Crassus. But he did have both of them working *for* him and committed to advancing his agenda. He gained access to their power, co-opting their accomplishments, resources, and influence to further his own goals.

Trust takes a long time to develop, and a savvy leader should look for ways to shorten the cycle time when they can. Through mutual value exchange, one leader can offer another a shortcut to developing trusted relationships with their teams or organizations. In Caesar's case, his powerful allies encouraged their followers to get behind him.

Eventually, Caesar earned the trust of his expanded circle by delivering genuine reforms.

Caesar's year in office was one of great tumult and violence. But when compared against years in which similar reforms were attempted, things were downright civil. Certainly, they were devoid of the wholesale slaughter that had marked senatorial suppression of reform agendas in the past. Caesar's ability to co-opt and leverage the power of others played a critical role in maintaining stability during a time of reform when people would rather have seen the whole system go down in flames. Commoners and soldiers considered him their friend and demonstrated a willingness to help him achieve his lofty goals. The loyalty went both ways. Caesar's power came from his support of the people around him. From the lowliest soldier to the loftiest senator, Caesar was always willing to engage in a quid pro quo for mutual benefit.

No matter how far he rose, Caesar always took care to connect with the people around him. Now, at the dawn of this next chapter in his career, it was paying extraordinary dividends.

7

PREEMPT YOUR ENEMIES

When pursuing change, leaders must often chart a course through turbulent waters. Furthermore, they must stay the course even when the team is scared or angry. During difficult times, anticipating the ways in which those resisting change will block progress and actively undermine their efforts is important. When the Senate suspended Caesar from office in 63 BC, he was able to undermine his enemies by acting in a way they did not expect. He preempted the Senate's attempt at marginalization and in doing so moved one step closer to implementing his reform agenda.

2&⁓

It is a sound that sends shivers down your spine and makes your hair stand on end. It is terrifying and primal: the cacophony of a mob. Hundreds of voices venting their anger and frustration, united to create a chorus of fear and destruction. The combined rage of a mob was one of the ancient world's most terrifying sights, and in the hands of an ambitious politician, it could be a truly deadly weapon.

It was 63 BC. Caesar had just been elected as *praetor*, a senior official in Rome one step removed from the consulship. Before he could even take office, the Senate, the members of which were suspicious of his populist motives, suspended him from his newly elected post. The people were furious.

Outside of his home in the heart of Rome, Caesar found a rioting mob bent on fighting for their rights and for him, the man who had become their champion. Impassioned, angry, and destructive, the mob came to Caesar's doorstep, ready for change, by any means necessary. Caesar stepped outside and stood before his people, carefully considering his words and how they would affect them, this pack of humanity pulsating with rage and ready to seek revenge on those who stood in Caesar's, and by extension their, way.

One has to wonder if Caesar felt a sense of satisfaction. The mob's very presence justified his course of action on behalf of the people and underscored his ambitious attempts at political reform. Caesar knew that it was not the moral superiority of the upper class that made Rome great; it was the hard work of the people. And for too long, the decision makers at the highest reaches of society had ignored those people's rights and interests. In his fight for reform, Caesar found obstacles at every turn, but at least he was still alive. Often those who attempted reforms were murdered by the Senate to prevent anyone from chipping away at its iron grip on the system. Caesar hadn't gotten far enough along to be a true threat . . . yet. But he was making inroads, and the Senate was getting suspicious of his progress.

If Caesar wanted to create change, then this was his opportunity. With his extraordinary rhetorical skills, he could whip the crowd into a frenzy and turn them loose against the senators. At this point in his turbulent career, this radical action would be Caesar's best opportunity to achieve his radical agenda. The Roman Republic was failing as a political institution; all the crumbling façade needed to collapse was someone bold enough—and with the right opportunity—to kick in the door.

Mobs were nothing new in Rome, and it wouldn't have been the first time a leader used mob violence to further a political agenda. Over the past few decades, many political disagreements had broken out in street fights, with factions arming their followers and cutting them loose in the city to destroy property and murder opponents. Now a mob had self-organized and presented itself to Caesar. Aware of the unique opportunity that had fallen into his lap, and looking to the people who had turned to him for marching orders, Caesar carefully considered what to do and what to say.

Having been thrown out of office by a contemptuous Senate, an ambitious man like Caesar may have been expected to unleash the mob and plunge Rome into another round of chaos and anarchy. Much to the surprise of the crowd, however, Caesar told them to disperse, to go home. He appreciated their support, but violence and destruction weren't the answer.

Think of Caesar as the sole member of a management team who understands that the success of the business is dependent on the employees. His goal, when he talked to the mob, was to do what was best for his people in the long run. He did not make his own issues and challenges the focus of the day; he stayed the course, doing what would benefit the long-term goals of the people.

Caesar understood the big picture at stake. If he had unleashed the crowd, then they would have caused great havoc and destruction. They might even have driven some of the particularly obstinate senators from Rome, giving Caesar the political window he needed to drive through his reforms. But that window wouldn't have stayed open forever. Such gains achieved through force would only have been temporary.

The elected offices in Rome turned over every year, and it was likely that an equally aggressive measure would be deployed in a year's time in order to restore the status quo. Plus, once back in control, the senators would seek revenge, bringing charges of sedition and treason.

Caesar knew that to effect lasting change, he would have to suffer the frustrations of driving his agenda through the existing legal structure. Using the force of the mob might change things on the surface, but it would do little to change the base of power on which the authority of the Roman government operated. Until Caesar could reform Rome's underlying structure, he had very little to gain and a lot to lose by using force to shortcut the process.

In this often-overlooked incident from Caesar's life and career, we get a unique window into the nature of force versus power. Many of his contemporaries struggled to see the difference, but Caesar clearly saw them as separate dimensions. What is more, he used this understanding as a guidepost for making decisions. The Senate sought to marginalize Caesar through their suspension. Setting the mob loose would have justified their action, proving that Caesar was a reckless maverick, unbound by the norms of civil society. Instead, they were shamed, one-upped by Caesar, as he demonstrated his deft understanding of power. He preempted the Senate's attempt at marginalization.

By declining the use of the mob as an instrument of revenge, Caesar avoided the trap that the Senate would have been able to use on him. He did not give the Senate ammunition to prove their scurrilous claims against him. Cowed, the Senate recalled Caesar to the Senate house. Leading men of the day took turns lauding Caesar for his actions, singing the praises of the man they had suspended from office just days earlier. They then voted to rescind the suspension and restore Caesar to his office.

Not only did Caesar retain his office, but also he got the upper hand with the Senate. By calming the mob down, he strengthened his connection to the people of Rome, and it was a bold demonstration to the Senate that he had a willing base of supporters committed to following his lead. In what was a supreme test of his leadership, Caesar emerged stronger than ever.

PREEMPT FROM A DISTANCE
THROUGH ALLIES

Leaders today can benefit from the proliferation of instantaneous ways to communicate across great distances, but it would be a risk to assume that speed of communication ensures quality and effectiveness. In Caesar's time, the long distances and slower and less reliable forms of communication forced careful planning and meticulous oversight to make sure that information was flowing freely and effectively.

Establishing lines of communication before they are needed, and making sure that key people are in the right places to advance policies and protect interests, is a vital step for any leader leaving the center of power. For Caesar, his post in the Gallic provinces left him and the reforms he had worked so hard to achieve vulnerable. Yet he was able to preempt his enemies by ensuring that he had people on the inside looking out for his best interests while he was away.

As consul, Caesar had succeeded in advancing land reform legislation. But now, as he prepared to take up his post as proconsul (governor) of the Gallic provinces, many greedy senators were all too ready to unwind the reforms. And so, before leaving for his foreign posting, Caesar took great care to establish lines of communication back to Rome. He set up correspondents to serve as his eyes and ears in the capital. What is more, Caesar, always going one step further, worked tirelessly to ensure that the next wave of elected officials included many who were aligned to his cause. Having the right people in the right posts deepened Caesar's ability to protect the hard-won gains he achieved.

As soon as he was off to the provinces, Caesar's detractors would fall upon his work and legacy and try to tear them to pieces. Caesar knew that he had to preempt their efforts to erode his hard work. He used his prestige and influence to ensure that qualified and well-intentioned people took over in the next wave of elections. He built a close-knit group of like-minded allies and actively fostered their collaboration and communication. These key successors and allies in the most important postings served as a check on senatorial hostility. Every time they made a move to undercut Caesar, these people were there as a bulwark.

Power is hard to gain and easy to lose. This essential truth has stood the test of time. Cultivating allies at all levels not only furthered Caesar's power base but also protected his flanks from those hostile to his cause. In today's increasingly global society, leaders are often required to spend time away from the center of power. Like Caesar, they must ensure that they have people on the inside looking out for their best interests while they are away.

PREEMPT FROM THE FRINGES

There is always a class of people on the outside looking in, and within this group, there is great opportunity to build and enhance power. The people you bring from outside of the power structure to the inside will be overwhelmingly grateful and loyal to you, the architect of their enfranchisement.

Caesar's courting of those on the edges of the social and political order most certainly grew his power base, but it also limited the future growth of the power of the competition, as the following story shows.

Once Caesar was on the road to his provincial assignment, it didn't take him long to start making waves. Fully aware of his sweeping ambitions, Caesar knew that he needed more disciplined legions to fight his upcoming campaigns. He took great care to draw his soldiers from the northern provinces, as they had just been granted full citizenship and thus were on the fringes of the political order. Most Roman leaders would have seen these people as being of only marginal utility. After all, they couldn't truly influence elections or carry much political clout. Traveling to Rome to cast a vote was a tall order for poor provincials, and many politicians of the old aristocratic order would turn up their nose at these outsiders. But Caesar saw something in them that his contemporaries didn't. Those on the fringes of a system carry fewer loyalties to existing figureheads. By recruiting in new territory, Caesar had little competition in winning their hearts and minds, and once established, the loyalty of these soldiers, and of the towns from which they came, would be ironclad.

The other benefit to Caesar's strategy of taking soldiers on the fringe under his wing was due to the rapidly changing Roman landscape. Roman hegemony was spreading, and so was the identity of what it meant to be Roman. It was only a matter of time before someone once considered a lowly provincial was just another Roman. Caesar's action of recruitment and patronage beat everyone to the punch. By the time the rest of his contemporaries caught up to Caesar's understanding of the evolving nature of the Roman identity, he had long since locked in the loyalty of this new group. Once again, he had preempted his adversaries.

A modern leader needs to anticipate the ways in which others will seek to erode his or her power. Success can come from preemptively defending a position or from avoiding the traps that competitors set. But tremendous power can also be gained through first-mover advantage when it comes to connecting with those at the margins of an organization. Extend the olive branch to those previously neglected, as Caesar did, and the breadth and depth of institutional support can soar.

8

INVEST IN YOUR POWER BASE

Building loyalty with people and within an organization takes time, action, and dedication. People freely give their power once they are motivated to follow a given leader. No matter how much we want people to want to follow us of their own free will, it takes time, discipline, and patience to become a leader with true power. It takes an investment in the organization around you.

Caesar never took his power for granted. He spent his life creating goodwill, incentives, and intrinsic motivation within those around him and the citizens at large. He nurtured his power as an asset and dedicated his career to the relationships with the people from whom he sought to derive power. What he did take for granted was his own safety. He would never think the Senate would stain its honor with the bloodshed of assassination within its halls; he let his guard down, and it cost him his life. But even in death, as this last story shows, his followers did not cease to feel loyalty, devotion, or obligation to the great leader. Even his death could be seen as one move closer to his ultimate goal of the transformation of the Roman system.

It was 44 BC. Caesar had come an extraordinary way. He had rebuilt his family's fortunes and cemented his personal legacy in the arc of one career. He had followed a different path and along the way heralded a new form of Roman leadership. Rather than using force and intimidation, Caesar used intrinsic motivation to find his way into the hearts and minds of the Roman people and upend the old system.

After the civil war ended, Caesar returned home to unusual peace. His enemies had fought and lost. Those who hadn't died in battle were pardoned. He had brought order to the world. Caesar stood alone at the top of the political heap, at the apogee of his power. Though still resentful of his power and prestige, the Senate voted to appoint him dictator for life. The word *dictator* means "ruthless autocrat" in the modern world. In the Roman system, a dictator was an appointed position, put into place only in deeply troubled times to steady the ship of state through enlightened and decisive action.

Caesar's next big move was to plan a war on the Parthians, a foreign empire to the east that had often bested Roman armies. As his planning reached a fever pitch, a group of increasingly desperate senators began plotting. Caesar's consolidation of power into a single person had sent many senators into a murderous rage. Politically impotent, they turned to force, and a few days before he was to leave for the Parthian campaign, a cabal of senators was determined to attack.

On the Ides of March, the Senate gathered within the Theater of Pompey. Caesar's former ally-turned-rival had built the magnificent edifice as the first stone theater in the city and as a monument to his glory. That morning, Caesar's wife awoke from a nightmare in which her husband had been assassinated. She begged him not to go to the Senate that day, and he took note of her warning. She was not prone to hysteria, and he prepared to send a message to the Senate, excusing himself due to poor health. But then one of the conspirators, Decimus Brutus, arrived at Caesar's home to ensure that he would attend the fateful meeting. He talked Caesar into attending the Senate meeting and accompanied Caesar to the theater. As Caesar made his way to the meeting, one of his allies, who had gotten word of the senatorial plot, frantically sent a dispatch to him to warn him. As Caesar arrived at the theater, he received the note and held it in his hand, but in the crush of senators moving in to attend the day's business, he didn't have the opportunity to open it.

Once the meeting was underway, the senators wasted little time. They advanced on the seated Caesar, stabbing wildly at the shocked leader. Quick to his feet, Caesar fought them off as best he could. But there were too many knives flying from all directions, and Caesar was soon fatally cut down. He bled to death on the floor, under the stoic, unmoving, and penetrating gaze of a marble statue of his long-dead archrival, Pompey the Great.

With their mission accomplished, the disorganized mob of slashing senators felt as though they had liberated the Roman people from a tyrant. In their minds, the death of Caesar was the liberation of the people and a triumph of the rightful power brokers over a cruel oligarch. Those who had conspired to bring about the death of Caesar , especially

Marcus Brutus, certainly portrayed this as the narrative. In their minds, Caesar had come to represent oppression, the destruction of ancient rights.

But what had they really accomplished? They had eliminated the most powerful individual in their world. The nature of this power meant that countless people had followed Caesar of their free will. This will was not so easily transferred. Caesar's death did not mean that the Senate could divvy up his power as they could the land of a conquered foreign foe. The Senate had savagely resorted to force to butcher a man they resented, but the power didn't just go away. It had to go somewhere. Where the conspirators felt that they had taken the initiative, events would prove how little command and control of the situation they really had.

The senators misread the situation; they failed to understand the concept of the power vacuum. Caesar had set to work consolidating the distributed power of the Roman world into his own hands. When he died, the power didn't simply diffuse itself; the system had changed, and the Senate had failed to account for this when they knifed Caesar to death on the Ides of March. It is a poignant lesson with multifaceted implications in today's context. Removing any leader or executive does not necessarily mean that their imprint on the organization goes away.

The Senate's use of force took away Caesar's life, but it didn't take away his power. Even in his death, the people of Rome rose to his support, sending the conspirators fleeing for their lives. Power always trumps force, and power carries a legacy. The conspirators failed to understand the difference. Caesar's murder on the Ides should be seen for what it was:

the complete failure of force. The Senate, so steeped in lofty rhetoric about liberty and tyranny, acted in the most tyrannical way of all by murdering someone because of ideological differences.

In the modern world of organizational politics, people often come into conflict with one another. In sizing up an antagonist, it's important to consider not only the individual but also the others from whom that individual has received power. The conspirators thought that by taking Caesar's life, they could take his power. They were wrong. In fact, the Senate's actions ended up costing them what little power and prestige they had left.

Though dead, Caesar had one more act that only increased the people's loyalty. In death, he proved that his dedication to them had been genuine. He cared deeply for them, and he rewarded their trust and affection. When Caesar's will was read, the people were astonished to discover that he left a sizable portion of his estate to the people of Rome. Overcoming the chronic debt that had hamstrung his earlier career, Caesar died an extremely wealthy man, and his act of generosity was a windfall for most Romans. Cash payments were to be made to every citizen of the city. His gardens and renowned art collection were to be donated to the people for their enjoyment and benefit.

The Senate had told the people that Caesar was a tyrant, a ruthless autocrat tamping down their rights and privileges, and had sought to sell the narrative that his death had liberated them. And yet, even in death, Caesar demonstrated his fealty to the people of Rome. Vanquished in life, Caesar triumphed in death. His bond to the people was secure. The

Senate would never again be the driving force of Roman politics. As the people of Rome considered their windfall, they reflected on the love they had for the fallen great man who had acted as their faithful servant. Truly, in Julius Caesar we find the first great example of servant leadership. While no such term existed in his day, it didn't need to: the people understood that he stood for them, and that he served their rights, needs, and interests.

But beyond the bequest to the people, Caesar's will had an even bigger shocker. He posthumously adopted his great-nephew Octavius and left the bulk of his estate to the mostly unknown young man.

INVEST IN YOUR SUCCESSORS

This choice of Octavius, which seemed strange to so many at the time, offers us critical insight into an issue central to the legacy of any leader: succession. Octavius was an unlikely successor to Caesar. Where Caesar was bold, charismatic, and courageous, Octavius was pensive, calculating, and enigmatic. He wasn't even considered a close relative. He was a great-nephew on his mother's side, far enough removed to barely be considered family. Worse of all, Octavius was just a teenager! Caesar had older familial and political associates with greater seasoning and experience. So why had he chosen Octavius?

While young and draped in what seemed to be yellow flags, Octavius had a few things going for him in Caesar's eyes. Octavius had a smoldering intelligence; he had a quick mind and demonstrated a deft understanding of the complex realities of Roman politics. Caesar understood that innate talents trump external flash. In seeking a successor, the brilliant Caesar valued someone who had the same intellectual abilities. Caesar also looked past social expectations. What other people thought didn't matter; what mattered was who would best honor and preserve Caesar's legacy. None of the other candidates would have come close.

Octavius also had a loyal circle of friends around him, including the astonishingly competent Marcus Agrippa and the witty and cultured Gaius Maecenas. Caesar knew that his choice of Octavius came with a group of people who would be loyal supporters, moderating the young man's impulses and helping him to make better, more measured decisions. In considering succession, Caesar demonstrated that one of the most important criteria is not just the candidate but also the people with whom that candidate is associated.

Unconventional though it may have been, Caesar's choice of successor proved truly inspired. Caesar broadened the criteria on which typical successor decisions were, and still are, made. He saw past age and conventions of relationships and the social context that came with Octavius. And young though Octavius was, it should be noted, Caesar was in his fifties; he should have had time to further nurture and mentor the young man. Caesar hadn't exactly expected to get murdered by a mob of senators.

On the day of his funeral, the people of Rome were restive. As the funeral oration was delivered, the combination of the people's love of Caesar and rage at his murder boiled over. The people began throwing sticks, furniture, and any fuel they could find onto Caesar's pyre, engulfing the Forum in flames. Much of Rome burned in the conflagration, which symbolized the eternal bond between Caesar and his followers. Truly, and quite literally, this last act of defiance on the part of the people forged in flames their relationship with their beloved leader.

The assassins were shocked. They had believed that they had liberated the people, and now those very people sought vengeance. The assassins fled for their lives, many barricading themselves as the citizens laid siege to their homes and laid waste to the city.

Caesar was truly beloved by the people of Rome. According to conventions of society, he should have had disdain for the common man, and they should have had disdain for him. He came from one of the most ancient and blue-blooded families in Roman society. Snobbery was his birthright: he was born at the very top of the social order in a society where social order meant everything. When you're born at the top, how much thought do you really give to the people beneath you?

EPILOGUE

In the course of human history, you would be hard-pressed to find someone more extraordinary than Julius Caesar. His combination of charisma, energy, vision, and ambition is truly unique. However, the world may not have taken note of his talent if Caesar hadn't uncovered a truth about leadership that evaded his contemporaries: it is the people that matter.

Caesar's unique relationship with the common people provided the foundation for his extraordinary career. Along the way, he set the tone for leadership from which we can learn today. Cutting through the fog and folklore of the centuries isn't easy. But if we look carefully, we can uncover the secrets that Caesar knew. We can adapt the style of one of history's most brilliant leaders to the modern world. And by doing so, we can take our organizations, and ourselves, to ever-greater heights, just as Caesar did for Rome.

Following the death of Julius Caesar, the Roman world again plunged into bloodshed and civil war. A second triumvirate formed among the dedicated lieutenants of Caesar. They united in avenging the death of their benefactor and then turned on one another. Through periodic warfare lasting more than a decade, Caesar's chosen successor, Octavius, emerged as the clear and sole victor. After consolidating his own power and securing his position atop the Roman order, he made a grand gesture of revoking all of his offices and returning to the Senate the keys of state. The senators reveled in their traditional prerogative at the center of public life. In 27 BC, to demonstrate their appreciation, they bestowed upon Octavius the honorific Augustus, or "revered one."

It was a sham. In the power vacuum that was created by the death of Caesar, Augustus spent years slowly winning for himself the power of his adoptive father. Despite his pretense of returning power to the Senate, he was firmly in charge. The Senate was ever after a hollow shell of its former self. The transformation of the Roman system was complete. The Roman Republic was dead. Gone forever. In its place rose the Roman Empire and, in the singular character of Augustus, the first emperor of Rome.

The senators' murder of Caesar sowed the seeds of their own demise and the collapse of the system they thought they were protecting. Even long after he was murdered, Caesar was still proving the triumph of power over force; the leadership genius of Julius Caesar rang loud and true.

Life in ancient Rome was just as complex and dynamic as it is today. Political fortunes rose and fell, values changed. Caesar's career is the story of adaptability, of the concept that power creates resilience.

Caesar might just have been history's greatest leader, and he managed change as well as anyone who has ever lived. In the chaotic modern world, when decision cycles are faster, consequences are greater, and the complexity is staggering, learning from the most adaptable leaders is all the more critical. In looking to the life and career of Julius Caesar, we have no example more germane to our world today.

In some versions of history, Caesar is portrayed as an autocrat: a ruthless politician who would step on anyone who got in his way in pursuit of his selfish goals. The reality is quite different. Caesar was a populist, more beloved by and supportive of the common citizen than anyone who had come before.

He was of the people, not above the people. In his life and career, he created a new paradigm of leadership; and along the way, he created the path to success for any leader in a complex organization. He did not use force. He did not compel followers through threats, fear, or intimidation. He understood the source of a leader's power: the incentive and desire for someone to follow of their own free will.

In Caesar's brilliant insight into the triumph of power over force, we find the invention of modern leadership. All of the qualities we seek in great leaders today—empathy, generosity, dedication to the people around them, commitment to the organization, and so much more—find their greatest example in Julius Caesar.

APPENDIX: CAST OF CHARACTERS

AHENOBARBUS (*Lucius Domitius Ahenobarbus*). An implacable foe of Caesar, Ahenobarbus pushed the Senate to resist the surge of Caesar's power, more from jealousy than from principle. Despite pushing Rome headlong into civil war through his anti-Caesar policies, Ahenobarbus was pardoned by Caesar for his actions.

ARIOVISTUS. A marauding German chieftain, Ariovistus was a formidable foe of Caesar and his army. Rising to meet the challenge, Caesar led his troops to legendary accomplishments, such as bridging the Rhine and invading Germany.

BRUTUS (*Marcus Junius Brutus*). Caesar looked after the young Brutus, son of a favorite mistress, and cultivated their relationship. Brutus's actions on the Ides of March have come down through history as the very definition of betrayal.

CAESAR (*Gaius Julius Caesar*). A brilliant leader seemingly full of contradictions, he was born a poor aristocrat and rose through the ranks as a defender of the common people and a radical reformer of the Roman system.

CATILINE (*Lucius Sergius Catilina*). A well-pedigreed aristocrat who had more ambition than talent, Catiline was accused of plotting a violent overthrow of the Roman Republic. Caesar was the sole voice who spoke up for leniency toward Catiline's hapless followers.

CATO (*Marcus Porcius Cato Uticensis*). Caesar's archnemesis, and the one guy who seemed to consistently get under Caesar's skin, Cato opposed Caesar at every turn, apparently out of spite. Cato ripped out his own intestines to prevent capture by Caesar, denying Caesar the chance to pardon his most ardent adversary.

CICERO (*Marcus Tullius Cicero*). Eloquent orator and cunning politician, Cicero was in many ways Caesar's opposite: from a humble background but a defender of the conservative prerogative.

CRASSUS (*Marcus Licinius Crassus*). Shadowy financier and subversive populist, Crassus backed Caesar early in his career and allied with him later, eventually joining with Caesar and Pompey in the First Triumvirate.

DECIMUS BRUTUS (*Decimus Junius Brutus Albinus*). A long-serving and highly capable lieutenant of Caesar, Decimus Brutus joined the conspiracy despite Caesar's devotion and patronage. On the Ides of March, Decimus convinced a reluctant Caesar to attend the Senate meeting, personally accompanying him to the gathering, and to his death.

MARC ANTONY (*Marcus Antonius*). Better suited as a lieutenant than a commander, Antony followed Caesar's lead but failed to establish himself as a leader in his own right. An aristocrat with a sense of entitlement, Antony was shocked and dismayed not to be chosen as Caesar's heir.

OCTAVIUS (*Gaius Octavius*). Caesar's great-nephew and surprising choice as heir, the quiet, calculating, and sickly youth eventually rose to the hallowed position of Rome's first and greatest emperor. Caesar saw clearly Octavius's genius even as the rest of the world had no idea who he was.

POMPEY (*Gnaeus Pompeius Magnus*). A brilliant organizer and accomplished self-promoter, Pompey was a man who had unsurpassed ambition in youth and demanded reverence as an adult. Dismissive of his younger rival, Pompey failed to appreciate the heights of Caesar's rise and the true depths of his power. Pompey died an inglorious death, beheaded at the command of the young Egyptian pharaoh Ptolemy XIII, brother and husband of Cleopatra.

VERCINGETORIX. Charismatic leader of the Gallic resistance, Vercingetorix rallied the fragmented tribes of Gaul in a united revolt against Roman domination. Captured and paraded in Caesar's triumph, Vercingetorix was ritually strangled in prison by a Roman soldier.

BIBLIOGRAPHY

Appian. *The Civil Wars*. Translated by John M. Carter. London: Penguin Books, 1996.

Beard, Mary. *SPQR: A History of Ancient Rome*. London: Profile Books, 2016.

Caesar, Julius, and Frederick Percy Long. *The Civil War*. New York: Barnes & Noble Books, 2005.

Cary, M. *A History of Rome: Down to the Reign of Constantine*. London: Macmillan, 1954.

Dando-Collins, Stephen. *Caesar's Legion: The Epic Saga of Julius Caesar's Elite Tenth Legion and the Armies of Rome*. Hoboken, NJ: John Wiley & Sons, 2004.

Everitt, Anthony. *Augustus: The Life of Rome's First Emperor*. New York: Random House, 2006.

Fuller, J. F. C. *Julius Caesar: Man, Soldier, and Tyrant*. Ware, Hertfordshire: Wordsworth Editions, 1998.

Gelzer, Matthias, and Peter Needham. *Caesar: Politician and Statesman*. Cambridge, MA: Harvard University Press, 1997.

Goldsworthy, Adrian. *Augustus: First Emperor of Rome*. New Haven, CT: Yale University Press, 2014.

———. *Caesar: Life of a Colossus*. New Haven, CT: Yale University Press, 2006.

Holland, Tom. *Rubicon: The Last Years of the Roman Republic*. New York: Doubleday, 2003.

Humphrey, John W., John P. Oleson, and Andrew N. Sherwood. *Greek and Roman Technology: A Sourcebook: Annotated Translations of Greek and Latin Texts and Documents.* London: Routledge, 1998.

Jiménez, Ramon L. *Caesar against the Celts.* Rockville Centre, NY: Sarpedon, 1996.

Laurén, Giles, and Francis W. Kelsey. *Caesar's Commentaries: The Complete Gallic War.* United States: Sophron Imprimit, 2012.

Meier, Christian. *Caesar: A Biography.* Translated by David McLintock. New York, NY: Basic Books, 1996.

Plutarch. Greek and Roman Lives. Translated by John Dry-den and Arthur Hugh Clough. Mineola, NY: Dover Publications, 2005.

Sallust. *The Jugurthine War/The Conspiracy of Catiline.* Translated and with an introduction by S. A. Handford. Harmondsworth: Penguin, 1963.

Strauss, Barry. *The Death of Caesar: The Story of History's Most Famous Assassination.* New York, NY: Simon & Schuster, 2015.

Suetonius. *The Twelve Caesars.* Translated by Robert Graves and J. B. Rives. London: Penguin Books, 2007.

Tacitus. *The Complete Works of Tacitus: The Annals; The History; The Life of Cnaeus Julius Agricola; Germany and Its Tribes; A Dialogue on Oratory.* Translated by Alfred John Church, William Jackson Brodribb, and Moses Hadas. New York: Modern Library, 1942.

ACKNOWLEDGMENTS

I would like to thank the following people, who have been incredibly helpful and supportive:

Above all, my wife, Erin, who supports me completely and yet challenges me to be better still.

My sons, Ethan and Everett, and my daughter, Harper, who demonstrate their own leadership genius every single day.

My parents, Kathy and Bruce Barlag, for whom there are not adequate words to express the depth of my gratitude and appreciation, and without whose support, none of this would be possible.

My sisters, Katie and Amy, and the guys lucky enough to have married them. We are a great team.

To my very dear grandparents, Bette and Bill Hoskins, who always set a shining example of what it means to have a generous spirit.

Jim, my partner in history, whom we all dearly miss, and Pat, for her excitement.

Ryan Masters, a stalwart friend and unconditional editor, always ready to help make everything better.

Trey Alverson, a terrific editor and a world-class friend, for his vision and passion for the subject, not to mention his countless hours of work in making this happen.

Antonio Fuertes Zurita, who has always been incredibly supportive and encouraging, particularly with this book.

Tom Conklin, professor, under whose guidance I went down the intellectual rabbit hole that led to this book.

Anthony Zolezzi, who has been a tireless supporter and great friend in everything, personal and professional, and who made me promise not to quit.

Pankaj Ghemmawat, who went above and beyond in offering advice, guidance, and friendship.

Jim Collins, for being even better than the best.

My agent, John Willig, for his energy and enthusiasm and for believing in this book from the beginning.

Keith Ferrazzi, for telling me that this was a good idea, even when I thought it was crazy.

Adam Grant, who is very much the real deal, giving even when he doesn't have to.

Doris Kearns Goodwin, a true source of joy in my life.

Charlene Lake, who has been much kinder to me than I deserve, and for a long time.

Jaap de Hoop Scheffer, a true statesman and a gracious human.

Charlene Wheeless, who reminds me of what it means to be exceptional.

Robert Norfleet, a mentor and friend for whom I could never begin to express adequate appreciation.

Filippo Passerini, who believes in this book and kept telling me to keep going.

Paul Polman, a leader changing the world for the better every day.

Jenn Cooper, whose exemplary notarial services inspire me to greatness.

ACKNOWLEDGMENTS

Bill Frerking, the one and only.

Robert Blackburn, whose generosity still makes me gasp.

Danielle Goodman, who helped me bring this thing together.

Elissa Rabellino, who helped make this a book of which I'm truly proud.

Andy Stefanovich and Courtney Ferrell, who poke, prod, and inspire me. Thank you for always bringing out my best.

And finally, a very special thanks go to Anna Leinberger, Neal Maillet, and Jeevan Sivasubramaniam, and the extraordinary team at Berrett-Koehler, for giving me a shot and then pushing me to do more than I could have thought possible. I love you guys.

INDEX

human nature,
    understanding of, 18–19
power base, 49, 66, 67, 69
    growing, 95
    investing in, 98–106
    successors, 104–106
power dynamics, 61
power vacuum, 102
praetor, 89–90
preempt your enemies. *See*
    enemies, preempting
proconsulship, 67–68, 94
pros and cons, 43, 59
    consulship story, 43–47

R
resentment, 19
resilience, 110–111
resistors, 64–66. *See also*
    enemies, political
return on investment, 50–52, 59
rhetorical ability, 34–35
Roman army
    Battle of Munda, 21–24
    as citizens, 10, 15
    as comrades, 16
    Mounted Tenth, 39–40
    revolt, 8–10, 16–17
Roman Empire, 110
Roman identity, 96
Roman Republic
    burning of Forum, 106
    civil war, 52–56, 58–59, 77–83
    consulship, 30, 43–47, 61,
        83–87
    governmental transition, 15
    land reform issue, 84–85, 94
    modern organization
        comparison, 49

ordinary Romans, 62–63, 78
reform needed, 48–49, 55–56
Rubicon River, 53–54, 57
rumors, 29–32, 48

S
safety net, 38–39
Second Triumvirate, 109–110
self-confidence, 55–58
senate, Roman, 4, 30–31
    consulship and, 44–47
    suspends Caesar from office,
        89–93
    tyranny, 102–103
senatus consultum ultimum
    (final act of the Senate), 52
servant leadership, 104
social order, 105–106
Spain, 81–83
stakeholders, communication
    with, 74
success
    communicating, 73–74
    organizational impact of,
        50–52
successors, 104–106
Sulla, 34

T
team, 21, 25, 37
    blame assignment and, 71
    focus, 69–70
    long-term goals, 91–93
    power and, 7, 10, 19
Tenth Legion, 39–40
Teresa, Mother, 19
Theater of Pompey, 100–101
tradition, 29, 37, 50–52, 83
tribunes, 52–53

ABOUT THE AUTHOR

 Phillip Barlag is an executive director at World 50, which initiates and facilitates the most interesting and influential business conversations in the world. He has the enormous privilege of serving remarkable leaders from some of the most well-respected companies around the globe.

Barlag has built numerous teams that have achieved remarkable success and economic growth. His career has also included lots of failure, procrastination, and getting himself in trouble. In all cases, Barlag has benefited from creative breakthroughs, and seeing both good and bad leadership first hand. His work explores the authentic nature of success and struggle in leadership.

His writing has been published in *Fast Company, MIT Sloan Management Review,* and a number of influential business blogs. He lives in the Atlanta, Georgia, area with his wife and three children.

Berrett–Koehler
Publishers

Connecting people and ideas
to create a world that works for all

Dear Reader,

Thank you for picking up this book and joining our worldwide community of Berrett-Koehler readers. We share ideas that bring positive change into people's lives, organizations, and society.

To welcome you, we'd like to offer you a free e-book. You can pick from among twelve of our bestselling books by entering the promotional code **BKP92E** here: http://www.bkconnection.com/welcome.

When you claim your free e-book, we'll also send you a copy of our e-newsletter, the *BK Communiqué*. Although you're free to unsubscribe, there are many benefits to sticking around. In every issue of our newsletter you'll find

- A free e-book
- Tips from famous authors
- Discounts on spotlight titles
- Hilarious insider publishing news
- A chance to win a prize for answering a riddle

Best of all, our readers tell us, "Your newsletter is the only one I actually read." So claim your gift today, and please stay in touch!

Sincerely,

Charlotte Ashlock
Steward of the BK Website

Questions? Comments? Contact me at bkcommunity@bkpub.com.

Certified

B

Corporation
bcorporation.net